English and American Furniture

ISBN: 978-0-9835784-9-9

Digitally Reproduced in 2012 by
CONVERPAGE Digital Reproductions
23 Acorn Street
Scituate, MA 02066
www.converpage.com

English and American FURNITURE

A PICTORIAL HANDBOOK OF FINE FURNITURE MADE IN GREAT BRITAIN AND IN THE AMERICAN COLONIES, SOME IN THE SIXTEENTH CENTURY BUT PRINCIPALLY IN THE SEVENTEENTH, EIGHTEENTH AND EARLY NINETEENTH CENTURIES

By

Herbert Cescinsky

Author of "English Furniture of the Eighteenth Century"; "Chinese Furniture"; "Early English Furniture"; "The Old World House, Its Furniture and Decoration."

and

George Leland Hunter

Author of "Decorative Furniture"; "Italian Furniture and Interiors"; "Decorative Textiles"; "Tapestries, Their Origin, History and Renaissance."

With More Than 400 *Illustrations*

TO THE MEMORY OF

GEORGE LELAND HUNTER

1867–1927

Who Contributed Much to Popular Understanding
of the Decorative Arts in America

PREFACE

THE credit for the scheme of the book is due to Henry W. Frohne, formerly Editor of Good Furniture Magazine. The photographs illustrating it are from the collection of the late George Leland Hunter who was to have carried the book to completion.

The original idea was of much wider scope, and had Hunter lived, there is no doubt that the book would have been larger and better. The plan which he outlined, to trace the development of furniture from the days of ancient Egypt up to the present day, illustrating examples not only from England and America, but also from the nations of antiquity, also from Italy, France and Germany, was an ambitious one, but George Leland Hunter was one who could have carried it out, as he possessed industry and erudition. The book which is now presented to the general public has been greatly contracted.

When Hunter's photographs and notes came to hand with the scheme of the book, the idea occurred to me that a simple handbook of furniture, in which native American and English examples were illustrated, side by side, might have an appeal, and it was all the book which I felt I was competent to write. I had the disadvantage that the valuable information which Hunter possessed of his photographed examples, had died with him. In addition, he had projected the illustration of modern-made American furniture (for which he had collected many examples) about which I knew nothing. These latter I have rejected, but I have been compelled to accept Hunter's photographs with any faults or inaccuracies they may possess. I had, nor have, no opportunity of examining the actual pieces themselves, but I have selected, to the best of my ability, examples which are true to their genus, as far as I could judge.

The book is intended for practical use, and stress is laid upon the comparative lesson which each example teaches, with as little of the academic and historical element as possible. To say how much I have missed the collaboration of George Leland Hunter is impossible. I have written the book as a stranger in a strange land, four thousand miles away from those aids, in the way of books, photographs and references, which tend to lighten the task of an author, but I have regarded the endeavor as a tribute to one whom the world of decoration and arts could ill spare, and I have performed it to the best of my ability.

H. C.

CONTENTS

ILLUSTRATIONS

CHAPTER II

GOTHIC AND TUDOR OAK FURNITURE

CHAPTER III

ENGLISH AND AMERICAN FURNITURE OF SEVENTEENTH CENTURY TYPE

CHAPTER IV

THE "WINDSOR" OR "TURNED" CHAIR

CHAPTER V

LACQUER WORK

CHAPTER VI

DEVELOPMENT OF THE ENGLISH WALNUT CHAIR

CHAPTER VII

ENGLISH AND AMERICAN MAHOGANY CHAIRS

CHAPTER VIII

AMERICAN AND ENGLISH DADO FURNITURE

CHAPTER IX

DOUBLE CHESTS, HIGH-BOYS AND CABINETS

CHAPTER X

SIDE TABLES, SIDEBOARDS AND COMMODES

CHAPTER XI

MAHOGANY TRIPOD FURNITURE

CHAPTER XII

OCCASIONAL TABLES

CHAPTER XIII

WALL FURNITURE OF THE EIGHTEENTH CENTURY

CHAPTER XIV

HEPPLEWHITE CHAIRS: ENGLISH AND AMERICAN

CHAPTER XV

WALL AND TOILET MIRRORS: AMERICAN AND ENGLISH

CHAPTER XVI

THOMAS SHERATON AND DUNCAN PHYFE

CHAPTER I

INTRODUCTORY

THERE are two ways in which this book could have been written; to divide it into two parts, English and American, or to contrast the work of the two nations in successive pages, showing the examples almost side by side. On consideration, I think the latter is preferable. One is enabled to point out the differences, and the resemblances, between English and American furniture when they are shown together; the lesson is easily learned and not readily forgotten.

It is necessary to begin with a truism; not all old furniture in the United States is of American origin, nor is the converse any more true; American-made pieces are to be found in England. The work of the two countries differs in three important particulars; the lumber used is not the same, there are certain traditions which are observed in the one country and not in the other, and the trade of the English furniture maker is divided in quite a distinct manner. Thus, in Great Britain are found the cabinetmaker, the chair-maker and the wood carver, all separate trades. None of the three would have been among the early emigrants, as they were not "general utility" men. It is the carpenter and the joiner who would be the most useful in the early American settlement, and there is no doubt that it was from the ranks of these men that the first settlers were culled. All trades have their traditions and methods, and to one acquainted with these, the hand of the carpenter, and not of the cabinetmaker, is evident in nearly all of the early American furniture, and even when the wood-working trade begins to segregate. In Philadelphia, in the last half of the eighteenth century, the traditions which arise are not those of the English cabinetmaker, chair maker or carver. This is not to say that they are less skilful or artistic; merely that they are distinct, and the Pennsylvania style—often loosely dubbed as "Chippendale"—is very different from any English work.

Up to almost the close of the seventeenth century, there is no parallel between the furniture of the two countries, and it is doubtful if much of the New England work was not imported from England. The attested native examples differ too widely in type and constructional method from others, apparently from the same locality, for this to be only a surmise.

Towards the middle of the eighteenth century there is a definite, and traceable, exodus of craftsmen from England, especially to Pennsylvania and Massachusetts. These men must have brought with them design books, plates, sketches or templates from England, as we know that either Chippendale's "Gentleman and Cabinetmaker's Director" (three Editions, 1754, 1755 and 1762) in its book form, or impressions from the plates (which may not have been the same thing, as there is some evidence to show that Thomas Chippendale's book was nothing more than a trade catalogue culled from the well-known patterns of his time) was in the hands of makers in Philadelphia in *circa* 1760. The trade card, or advertisement, of Benjamin Randolph, was a composite of some seven or eight plates from the "Director," literally copied. But for a misunderstanding about English tea in Boston Harbor in 1775, Philadelphia might have had a Chippendale's "Director" of its own, as, in that year, a prospectus was issued of "The Gentleman and Cabinetmaker's Assistant" (dangerously near a plagiarism) by "the ingenious Mr. Folwell" of that city, which was to consist of sketches and designs, with instructions for making. Apparently, the book never progressed beyond the prospectus stage, and there is no evidence to show that a single drawing or design was ever made for it. That year was to hear the sound of rifle volleys at Bunker Hill; the next to witness the Declaration of Independence. In 1778 came the alliance with France, and in 1781 Cornwallis surrendered at Yorktown. In 1789 the Constitution of the United States was adopted. War with England was again declared in 1812. Here are six valid reasons against the success of such a publishing venture. These incidents serve to show the effect which history and political events may have on the styles in furniture and decoration of a country. Perhaps this is the reason why the English models of the later eighteenth century were never literally copied in the eastern states, and why so-called "Philadelphia Chippendale" differs, in such a marked degree, from its English prototypes.

This book is, primarily, what its title states; a handbook.

The text is kept as brief, and as full of facts, as possible. There are many other books (my own among the number) where the subjects, herein referred to, are stated at greater length and in full detail, and those who desire closer acquaintance with a vast subject, can be referred to those volumes. This is a book for the busy man, for those who wish to assimilate something of English and American furniture in a short time. It is designed to act as a handbook for ready reference. This introductory chapter, therefore, is only a leisurely preamble before entering on the actual subject itself, succinctly, but in adequate detail. It is hoped, also, that the reference tables of events, dates and craftsmen, and the glossary in the concluding pages, may be found of some assistance to that busy man.

CHAPTER II

GOTHIC AND TUDOR OAK FURNITURE

CARPENTER AND ARKWRIGHT

THE Gothic period, in furniture, may be said to extend from the thirteenth to the middle of the sixteenth centuries and persists for over forty years after the Renaissance had been introduced into England, either direct from Italy, or transmitted through France and the Low Countries.

In the fifteenth century, the important wood-worker was the carpenter, who was responsible for such important works as timber roofs, half-timber houses, screens and churches and cathedrals, pulpits, font covers, choir stalls and similar works of importance. Of actual furniture, he made very little, probably because it may have been beneath his dignity to descend to prosaic pieces such as cupboards, chests, stools or tables. The chair was a piece of the highest importance and rarity until about the end of the sixteenth century, and very few examples exist prior to 1600.

This being a handbook of furniture, only such examples are illustrated as one can reasonably expect to find in the market; and this excludes practically all early carpenter-made furniture. In the sixteenth century, if not before, the maker of household furniture was of an inferior grade, known as "arkwright," a term which can be understood when it is explained that chests were always referred to as "arks," and the "wright" has survived in the name of "wheelwright" and "shipwright." This arkwright furniture is rare, but it can be met with, occasionally, and, therefore, some examples are illustrated here. The wood is nearly always oak, *Quercus rubrum,* and of English growth, but occasionally poplar or deal were used. Walnut was an unknown wood, in England, at this period.

DISSOLUTION OF MONASTERIES

IT WAS in *circa* 1525 that Henry VIII began to suppress and destroy the great monasteries, which were the homes of all the artistic crafts of England, and had been since the Middle Ages.

The monks and lay brethren were driven forth as outlaws and outcasts, and, at one stroke, were destroyed the Gothic arts in England. The cultured of the next generation turned to the new manner, the Renaissance; only the untutored remained faithful to the Gothic of their youth, dimly remembered, and with all the early fine principles misunderstood. The result is that in constructive skill, this post-dissolution Gothic is far behind the Renaissance work of the same period. Doors are mere pierced slabs of wood; not framed and mortised in the skilled manner of the carpenter. To this date belong the so-called chip-carved chests, where the design is patterned with the divider and chiseled with the gouge. Occasionally Renaissance motives, such as heads enclosed in circular cartouches, or similar crude ornament, is attempted, but with dubious success.

This Gothic oak furniture has no parallel pieces of American origin, for obvious reasons, and has been briefly referred to here, in text and illustration, in consequence. While of no great artistic merit, it has a considerable value, due to its extreme rarity.

TUDOR FURNITURE

THE Tudor furniture is almost as rare, but, due to ignorance or the desire to increase the market value of a piece by antedating it, many characteristic early seventeenth century examples are referred to as "Elizabethan." There is one exception to this, that is in the instance of the "turneyed" (turned) or "thrown"* chairs; those produced entirely on the lathe. We know that these chairs existed in the sixteenth century, as they are referred to in inventories of the time, but none appear to have survived, due, in all probability, to their fragile construction. They were freely copied in the seventeenth century, and, possibly, with great fidelity, therefore, while they are really seventeenth century in actual date, they are sixteenth in type, and, hence of great interest to the collector.

The Tudor chair, until the close of the sixteenth century, is always of the one kind, a box with a back and arms. The chair with legs belongs to the Stuart period. Similarly with the table and the stool. Prior to about 1570 these are invariably of the trestle-end type. The Gothic table was a huge affair, but furniture begins to become lighter, both in timber and construction, towards the end of the Tudor period.

*"Throwing" is the mediæval term for turning.

LIVERY CUPBOARD, MID-16TH CENTURY. DOORS ARE MERE PIERCED SLABS OF WOOD, CRUDE ARKWRIGHT CONSTRUCTION

LIVERY CUPBOARD, THE WORK OF THE ARKWRIGHT, MID-16TH CENTURY

CUPBOARD PROBABLY FROM NORTHERN FRANCE. MID-16TH CENTURY WORK OF A CARPENTER

DOLE CUPBOARD OF THE MID-16TH CENTURY. THE REMEMBERED "GOTHIC" OF THE ARKWRIGHT

OAK CUPBOARDS FROM ENGLAND AND FRANCE

(LEFT) TWO-TIER CUPBOARD WITH LINENFOLD PANELS. CARPENTER MADE, LATE *16*TH CENTURY

(BELOW) CHEST OF EARLY *14*TH-CENTURY TYPE SHOWING DAWN OR THE GOTHIC DETAIL OF THE ARKWRIGHT

DEBASED ARKWRIGHT TYPE OF CHEST OF MID-*16*TH CENTURY WITH CRUDE FRENCH RENAISSANCE DETAILS

ENGLISH OAK CUPBOARD AND CHESTS

CREDENCE TABLE WITH REVOLVING HINGED TOP. TYPE OF LATE 16TH CENTURY WITH FRENCH RENAISSANCE DETAIL

THE OLDEST AMERICAN TABLE, ILLUSTRATING THE GOTHIC TRESTLE-TYPE OF CONSTRUCTION

TWO OAK TABLES

OAK CHAIR, TUDOR TYPE OF *c. 1520* WITH FINE CONSTRUCTION AND CORRECT GOTHIC DETAIL. THE WORK OF THE CARPENTER

ENGLISH OAK CHAIR OF 16TH CENTURY

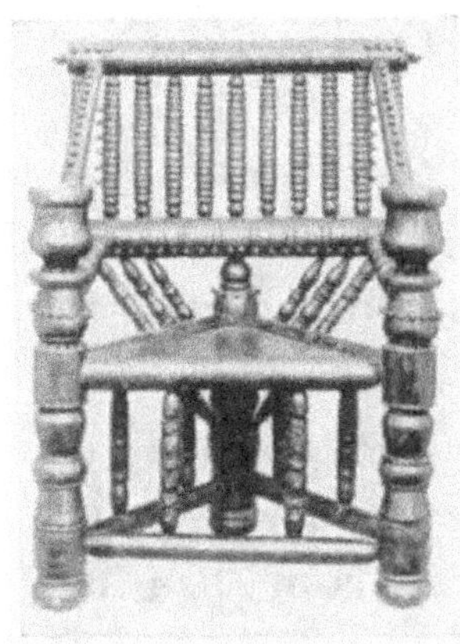

"TURNEYED" CHAIR IN OAK, ELM AND OTHER WOODS, PROBABLY LATE 16TH CENTURY

BOX TYPE CHAIR OF LATE 16TH CENTURY BEFORE DEVELOPMENT OF CHAIRS ON LEGS

THE "GLASTONBURY" CHAIR, EARLY 17TH CENTURY. USUALLY DESCRIBED AS 16TH CENTURY

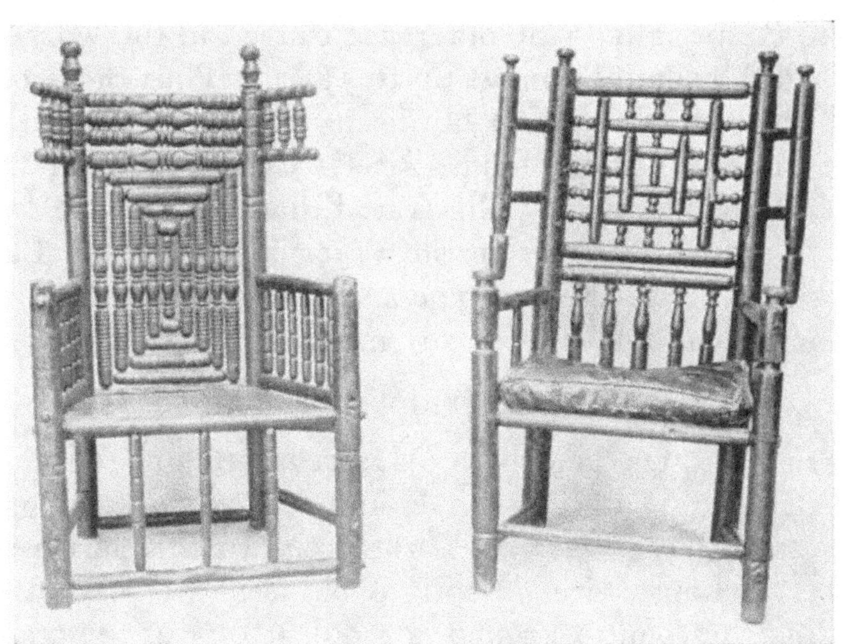

"TURNEYED" CHAIRS OF OAK, ELM, YEW AND FRUIT-WOOD, 17TH CENTURY COPIES OF 16TH CENTURY ORIGINALS

ENGLISH OAK CHAIRS OF 16TH AND 17TH CENTURIES

CHAPTER III

ENGLISH AND AMERICAN FURNITURE OF SEVENTEENTH CENTURY TYPE

FURNITURE STYLE IN THE EARLY COLONIES

IN ANY new settlement, the important articles of furniture, that is, those which would be first made, would be chairs and tables. Chests and cupboards could wait until a leisure time. Robinson Crusoe, on his island, never achieved either, it will be remembered. Thus, in the New England Colonies, it is to chairs and tables which one would turn to find copies from English models, if any such existed at all. We must bear in mind that these would be the work of the carpenter, not of the cabinet or chair-maker, for reasons which have already been stated, and not only would one expect variations on this account alone, but also the characteristics of the districts from which the early settlers had emigrated would be followed where practicable.

In chairs, especially, wide difference existed in the work of the various English counties, almost up to 1680. Thus those of Lancashire, Yorkshire, the Welsh bordering counties, Warwickshire, Cheshire, and the districts immediately around London vary in important details more easily illustrated than described. In addition, the "Windsor" chair from the Wycombe district in Buckinghamshire would be a persistent type, as these chairs had a long tradition behind them, and were easily made.

NO WALNUT PERIOD IN AMERICA

THE Pilgrim Fathers landed in Massachusetts in 1620, fleeing from the persecution of Charles I, and the exodus was greatest from Lancashire and Western Yorkshire. In the parish church of Chorley, in Lancashire, is still to be seen the pew of Miles Standish, and the country around is redolent of Puritan traditions to this day. The new colony was further reinforced by Roundhead emigrants who left England when the monarchy was restored in 1660. It is only after this date that New England begins to develop a distinctive style of its own, in oak furniture, at the time when walnut was becoming the fashionable furniture wood in England. Herein lies the chief distinction between the English and

American work of the later years of the seventeenth century, and as Philadelphia was only in the making at the time, if even commenced, "American" furniture is that of the New England states only. Walnut comes into fashionable (but not general) use after 1660 in England, whereas oak is the American timber until mahogany replaces it. There is really no walnut period in America, although the wood was used, sparingly, especially on the banks of the Delaware.

On the other hand, in England, walnut was the wood for chairs, tables and similar pieces, whereas oak still persisted for panelings and wall-pieces. Walnut wainscotings are not unknown but they are exceedingly rare, while mahogany never appears to have been used for this purpose at any time. Perhaps the reason is that panelings were the work of the carpenter at all periods in English woodwork, and oak was his favorite timber. The wall-pieces, court and standing cupboards of the late seventeenth century were also in his hands, and it is only in the last years of William III that the cabinetmaker is responsible for all furniture, chairs and kindred pieces alone excepted.

GETTING AWAY FROM ENGLISH MODELS

It is from 1640 to nearly 1700 that the English pieces are the most faithfully copied in New England (due allowance being made for want of facilities and of trade traditions), but here it is often the case that the American models are anything from twenty to fifty years behind the current fashions in England, and, in dating of examples, due allowance must be made for this fact. There is always a certain crudity, more in line and proportion than in actual workmanship, which enables one to distinguish the American furniture of this period, whereas, in the last half of the eighteenth century, definite styles had been established, especially in Rhode Island and in Pennsylvania, and the resemblances to English models are then more imaginary than real. The timber itself is, of course, some indication of origin (in fact, it is the best of all criteria), but in photographs or book illustrations this guide cannot exist, for obvious reasons.

ENGLISH STOOLS, CHAIRS AND TABLES

Even up to the walnut period in England, so long as hospitality in the greater houses was on a lavish and elastic scale, the stool retained its popularity as the usual seat for meals, especially in the home or southern counties, but to accommodate the extravagantly hooped skirts which were general among the better class women at this period, chairs without arms became general in the Midlands, especially in Lancashire and Yorkshire, each of which developed its own definite type. Examples of both are illustrated here and are easily recognizable.

The progression of the English oak table also requires some explanation. The Tudor type was of the end-trestle form, almost until the end of the reign of Elizabeth, when the bulbous leg came into vogue. This persisted almost until the close of the Stuart dynasty, but shortly after the Restoration the vase or baluster turning began to replace it for large tables, and the spiral or twist (copied from the chair-maker) for those of smaller size. In the Commonwealth days the so-called bobbin-turning had a short lease of fashion, and, with the first years of the eighteenth century, the cabriole was introduced from Holland. It is found, in embryonic form, in the William and Mary pieces, but, as a rule, the plain smooth cabriole is an innovation of the first years of the reign of Anne.

AMERICAN FURNITURE WOODS

THE principal furniture woods of the New England states (the home of these Americanized models of the English seventeenth century) were oak and maple. In rare instances walnut is found, but for chairs, elm, ash, hickory and plane tree are more common. For furniture of the settler or cottage type, deal and pine were often used, and one frequently finds pieces where many woods are used together. Veneering is rare, and when found, the base is usually soft pine (after the Dutch manner) instead of the English oak. It is more than probable that some of this furniture may have originated from New York State and even from what is now the New Jersey shore to the north of the Schuylkill and the Delaware, and up to Albany.

Localities are difficult to fix, as the unsettled state of the country would cause frequent migrations from place to place anywhere from the Hudson to the Charles River, and the term "New England" is perhaps the best to designate much of this American furniture of seventeenth century type. The presence of heavy wall pieces, such as the court or standing cupboard would indicate a more or less fixed settlement where the early colonists were firmly entrenched in these homesteads and guarded by forts or stockades.

LANCASHIRE TYPE, *c. 1670*

YORKSHIRE TYPE, *c. 1680*

EARLY YORKSHIRE TYPE, *c. 1625*

WAINSCOT CHAIR, *1650–60*

ENGLISH OAK CHAIRS

c. 1625

c. 1630

c. 1650

ENGLISH OAK STOOLS

MIDLAND TYPE, *c. 1650*

WELSH BORDERING COUNTIES TYPE, *c. 1640*

EAST ANGLIAN TYPE, *c. 1650.* (THE ROCKERS ARE ADDITIONS)

CHESHIRE OR WARWICKSHIRE TYPE, *c. 1640.* (FEET AND UNDERFRAMING MISSING)

ENGLISH OAK CHAIRS

CHILD'S OAK CHAIR, *c. 1660*

PAINTED BEECH CHAIR, JAMES II, *1685–9*

PAINTED BEECH CHAIR, POSSIBLY DUTCH. THE EMBRYONIC CABRIOLE LEG. *c. 1695*

DAY BED OF BEECH AND WALNUT, *c. 1685*

VARIOUS ENGLISH CHAIRS

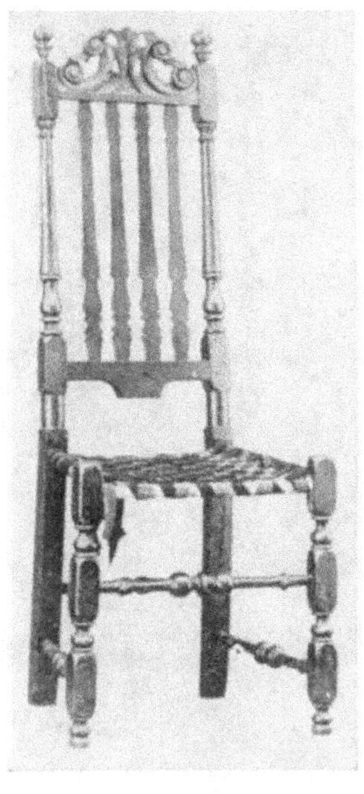

MAPLE CHAIR, ENGLISH TYPE OF *1680*. *c. 1710–20*

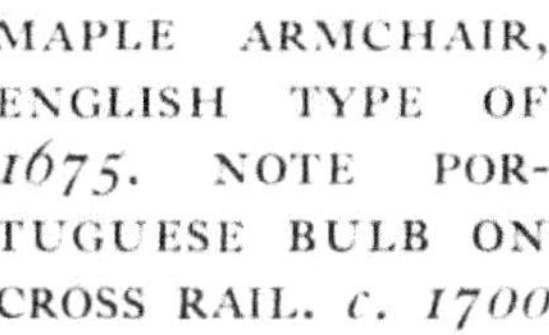

MAPLE ARMCHAIR, ENGLISH TYPE OF *1675*. NOTE PORTUGUESE BULB ON CROSS RAIL. *c. 1700*

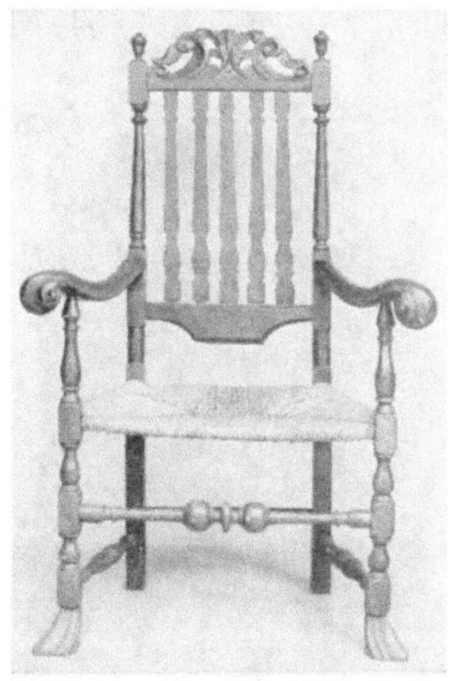

MAPLE, ASH AND OAK ARMCHAIR, ENGLISH TYPE OF *1670* WITH SPANISH WHORLED FEET. *c. 1700*

MAPLE ARMCHAIR, ENGLISH OR DUTCH TYPE OF *c. 1680*. EMBRYONIC SPANISH FOOT. *c. 1700*

NEW ENGLAND CHAIRS OF 17TH CENTURY TYPE. THE BALUSTER BACKS ARE ALL FLAT IMITATIONS OF TURNING

MAPLE CHAIR, *18*TH CENTURY HOOPED BACK, FIDDLE SPLAT WITH BULB AND SPANISH FOOT, *c. 1680*

MAPLE ROCKING CHAIR WITH RUSH SEAT, COMBINATION OF ENGLISH TYPES FROM *c. 1650* TO *1690*. PROBABLY *1720*

MAPLE CORNER CHAIR WITH RUSH SEAT. SPANISH FOOT IN COMBINATION WITH TURNED RAILS OF WINDSOR CHAIR, *c. 1725*

MAPLE CHAIR. *17*TH AND *18*TH CENTURY DETAILS. *c. 1730*

NEW ENGLAND CHAIRS OF 17TH AND 18TH CENTURIES

AMERICAN-ENGLISH MIDLAND TYPE. *c. 1675*

AMERICAN-ENGLISH SOUTHWEST COUNTY TYPE. *c. 1670*

NEW ENGLAND OAK CHESTS

AMERICAN-ENGLISH EAST ANGLIAN TYPE. *c. 1670*

OAK AND PINE CHEST WITH INCISED AND INLAID DECORATION, DATED *1705*

NEW ENGLAND OAK CHESTS OF CREDENCE TYPE

OAK CHEST, CONNECTICUT VALLEY TYPE, *c. 1690*

OAK CHEST, MASSACHUSETTS TYPE (SALEM). *c. 1705.* THE INTRICATE MITERING OF MOULDINGS AND SPLIT BALUSTERS COPY THE ENGLISH OF *c. 1685*

NEW ENGLAND CHESTS WITH APPLIED SPLIT-BALUSTER ORNAMENTS

PINE CHEST, PROBABLY LATE *17*TH CENTURY

OAK CRADLE, *c. 1640.* THIS PIECE MAY HAVE BEEN IMPORTED FROM LANCASHIRE

NEW ENGLAND FURNITURE

CARVED AND INLAID. *c. 1660.* THE ELABORATE EAST ANGLIAN TYPE

ENGLISH OAK COURT CUPBOARD

EAST ANGLIAN TYPE OF *1630–40*

ENGLISH OAK COURT CUPBOARD

CUPBOARD FORMERLY THE PROPERTY OF CHARLES R. WATERS OF SALEM, *c. 1650.* TURNED BALUSTERS AND ORNAMENTS STAINED BLACK AND EBONYED BALL FEET. *63½* INCHES HIGH

NEW ENGLAND OAK COURT CUPBOARD

BOSTON OR SALEM, *c. 1660*

NEW ENGLAND OAK COURT CUPBOARD

BORROWED FROM ENGLISH LANCASHIRE TYPE OF *c. 1650*

CONNECTICUT VALLEY OAK COURT CUPBOARD

OAK AND DEAL COURT CUPBOARD, ELABORATELY MITERED MOULDINGS AND APPLIED SPLIT BALUSTERS. *c. 1670*

OAK COURT CUPBOARD, MOULDINGS AND BOSSES PAINTED BLACK AND RED. *c. 1690*

NEW ENGLAND CUPBOARDS

NEW ENGLAND OAK AND DEAL CUPBOARD. LOWER PART IN FORM OF CHEST WITH DRAWERS. *c. 1700*

NEW ENGLAND PINE GRAINED CORNER CUPBOARD, EARLY *18*TH CENTURY. SPLIT BALUSTERS APPLIED AS PILASTERS

NEW ENGLAND CUPBOARDS

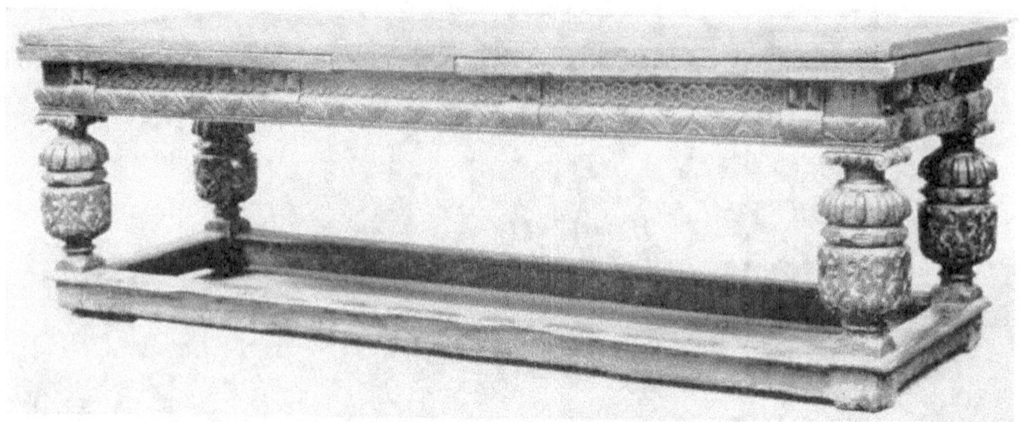

OAK DRAW TABLE (THE CAPPING TO THE UNDER RAILS IS NOT ORIGINAL). EAST ANGLIAN TYPE

OAK REFECTORY TABLE, MIDLAND TYPE. NOTE THE CRUDITY AS COMPARED WITH THE EXAMPLE ABOVE

ENGLISH OAK TABLES, TYPE OF FIRST QUARTER OF THE 17TH CENTURY

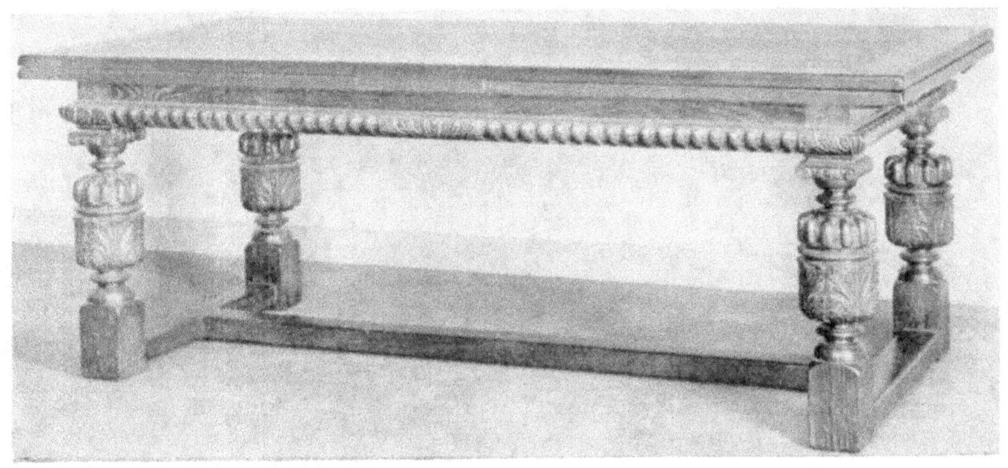

THE H-TYPE OF STRETCHER WAS NEVER USED IN THE *17*TH CENTURY

SUPPORTED ON TWO BULBOUS LEGS WITH CROSS-SHAPED FEET. TABLES OF THIS KIND ARE VERY RARE IN ORIGINAL STATE

REPRODUCTIONS OF ENGLISH OAK 17TH CENTURY TABLES

OAK TABLE WITH BALUSTER-LEGS AND CARVED RAIL. THE DATE *1697* IS NOT ORIGINAL. TABLES OF THIS KIND BELONG TO THE WALNUT YEARS OF ENGLISH CHAIRS AND TO THE POST-RESTORATION PERIOD

OAK BALUSTER-LEG TABLE WITH MOULDED FRAMING AND STRETCHER. THE SIMPLE REFINED TYPE OF *c. 1670*

ENGLISH OAK TABLES OF BALUSTER-LEG TYPE FROM 1660–1685

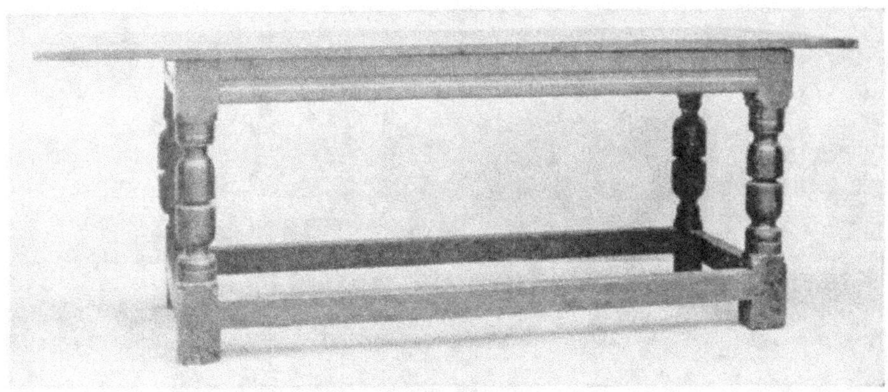

1660–70. THE FINAL ATTENUATION OF THE EARLY STUART BULBOUS LEG

OAK "SUFFOLK" LOW DRESSER, *c. 1690.* THIS PIECE BELONGS TO THE POST-RESTORATION WALNUT YEARS OF THE ENGLISH CHAIR

ENGLISH OAK SIDE TABLES OF THE 17TH CENTURY

LATE *17*TH CENTURY TYPE OF GATE TABLE WITH "BUTTERFLY" BRACKETS USUALLY FOUND IN MAPLE, HICKORY OR DEAL

ANOTHER TYPE OF "BUTTERFLY" FLAP TABLE OF *17*TH CENTURY PATTERN

AMERICAN FLAP TABLES, MAPLE AND CHESTNUT

MAPLE "BUTTERFLY" FLAP TABLE

HINGED-TOP TABLE WITH PIVOTED "BUTTERFLY" BRACKETS. MASSACHUSETTS LATE *17*TH CENTURY

MAPLE AND PINE TABLE WITH BOBBIN-TURNED LEGS. NEW ENGLAND LATE *17*TH CENTURY

TRIANGULAR FLAP MAHOGANY TABLE, ABOUT *1750*. THE *17*TH CENTURY TYPE PERSISTING

AMERICAN GATE-LEG AND FLAP TABLES OF LATE 17TH CENTURY TYPE

WALNUT AND OAK GATE-LEG TABLE WITH SINGLE "GATE." ENGLISH, *c. 1680–90*

WALNUT GATE-LEG TABLE WITH DOUBLE GATE AND BALUSTER AND BOBBIN-TURNING. NEW ENGLAND LATE *17*TH CENTURY, PROBABLY *1700*

ENGLISH AND AMERICAN GATE-LEG TABLES

OAK TABLE WITH BOBBIN-TURNING, ABOUT *1670*

BOX TABLE WITH LID. MAPLE AND OAK. LATTER HALF OF *17*TH CENTURY

MAPLE AND PINE TABLE, *c. 1700*

WALNUT TABLE WITH SINGLE GATE BOBBIN-TURNED LEGS. THIRD QUARTER OF *17*TH CENTURY

AMERICAN TABLES OF OCCASIONAL TYPE

OAK AND WALNUT TABLE, ENGLISH. EARLY RESTORATION TYPE WITH SPIRAL-TURNED LEGS AND RAILS, *c. 1670*

OAK TABLE WITH ONE FLAP AND SINGLE GATE. ENGLISH, PROVINCIAL, *c. 1700*

TABLE OF CHERRY WOOD. NEW ENGLAND, LATE *17*TH OR EARLY *18*TH CENTURY

MAPLE TABLE. NEW ENGLAND, LATE *17*TH CENTURY

ENGLISH AND AMERICAN TABLES OF THE LATE 17TH CENTURY FOR COMPARISON

WALNUT VENEERED TABLE, POSSIBLY NEW AMSTERDAM COPYING LATE *17*TH CENTURY DUTCH MODEL

CHERRY WOOD TABLE COPIED FROM THE EXAMPLE ON THE LEFT. SALEM OR BOSTON, FIRST QUARTER OF THE *18*TH CENTURY

BOX TABLE OF CHESTNUT AND VARIOUS WOODS. CRUDE NEW ENGLAND (PROBABLY CONNECTICUT VALLEY) TYPE OF *c. 1670*

AMERICAN TABLES, VARIOUS TYPES

WALNUT TABLE, ENGLISH, WITH INVERTED CUP-TURNED LEGS AND WAVY STRETCHER. THE TYPE INTRODUCED FROM HOLLAND, IN THE REIGN OF WILLIAM III, *c. 1695*

DEAL AND WALNUT TABLE WITH CUP-TURNED LEGS AND STRETCHERS. AMERICAN COPY OF THE ENGLISH WILLIAM AND MARY ABOVE, *c. 1700–20*

ENGLISH AND AMERICAN LATE 17TH CENTURY SMALL TABLES OF THE ORANGE WALNUT YEARS

CHERRY WOOD TABLE. CONNECTICUT, LATE 17TH CENTURY

PINE AND WALNUT TABLE. EARLY 18TH CENTURY COPYING THE ENGLISH LATE 17TH CENTURY TYPE

NEW ENGLAND TABLES

CHAPTER IV

THE "WINDSOR" OR "TURNED" CHAIR

STYLE DEVELOPMENT IS GRADUAL

THE furniture of both England and America has centuries of tradition behind it. If we take any piece, however original or novel it may appear to be, it will be found that it has sprung, wholly or in part, from a long ancestral line. In the majority of instances, there is a continual change; an evolution, but the "bridgepieces" exist, if we search for them patiently, and are not too eager to establish a theory, and, in consequence, to ignore examples as "sporadic," which conflict with our preconceived notions. In the sense that all worth-while development is gradual, it is literally true that a new style has never existed in English furniture, and the same is true of American. At no period did a population awake one morning to hail a new manner. From Gothic right up to Sheraton or Duncan Phyfe there is this developmental line, almost unbroken. Occasionally some new and drastic circumstance may impose a new and rigid channel into which evolution is forced, in the same way as the zoning law in New York compelled architects to design high buildings in such a manner that, after a certain number of stories, they were obliged to step back and so produce a series of receding planes. In other words, a new era in building design appeared to supervene, where masses were conceived vertically instead of as a series of horizontals—yet the pyramids of ancient Egypt were built in much the same manner. There is nothing new under the sun.

In something like the same way, we do get certain radical changes, not only in form but also in method, when walnut begins to supersede oak, shortly after 1660, and walnut, in turn, is ousted by mahogany in *circa* 1725. In these years there is a trend away from solid construction to veneering, then back to the solid again in the first mahogany years, and a reversion to veneering again when the rare figured mahoganies begin to be imported. At no period, however, is the change a sudden one. We have seen how oak persists in the walnut period, and chairs and other pieces, in the full manner of the Chippendale school, but in walnut, are by no means exceptional.

WOOD HAS ITS LIMITATIONS

ONE point here is of great importance. No furniture which has any artistic permanence, and which fills its gap in the evolutionary sequence, can be, or ever was, designed by one unacquainted with the limitations of timber or the methods of the wood-worker. Thus, a cabinetmaker-designed table has an overhanging top, invariably. Why? Because it is in the nature of wood to shrink, and with an overhang of an inch or two, a fractional shrinkage is not noticeable, and does not affect the stability of the piece. It is only the "original" designer who projects a table with a top flush with the framing, and where the slightest contraction becomes a glaring defect, immediately. One is practical; the other is not. One is apt to forget that a piece of furniture is not purely ornamental; it has a definite function to fulfil, if only to stand upright and firm. The impractical "original" designer can no more take liberties with the designing of a chair than he can with an automobile. The one will not function as a chair, nor the other travel as a motor car. It may be urged that the latter is purely a piece of mechanism and, as such, must be mechanically perfect also. The only difference is that while one can "get away" with an uncomfortable and badly-designed chair under the holy names of "art" and "creation," it is difficult to sell an automobile which will not go.

WINDSOR CHAIRS HAVE CHANGED LITTLE

IN MUCH the same way as with biological evolution where certain types develop rapidly and others remain practically stationary (the tortoise and the shark are both much the same as they were millions of years ago), we have an instance in both English and American furniture, in the chair which is produced on the lathe almost entirely, the "turneyed" or "Windsor" chair. For hundreds of years, literally, in the woods and forests of Buckinghamshire, the wood turner, with his primitive pole or bow-lathe, would cut down his timber, and in its unseasoned state, more or less, produce his chairs entirely by turning, the seats alone excepted. For the latter he used elm, a timber which can hardly be improved by any seasoning or drying as it absorbs moisture at any and all times, and for the bows of his backs, the shaped arms and the splats, he cut the wood which, for ages, had been consecrated to other bows, those which sent the cloth-yard shaft in battle—English yew. Properly used, this is a beautiful wood, and the variety which usually grows in churchyards was the most esteemed, perhaps for a ghoulish reason.

Yew tree bends readily, does not spring, warp or split, and takes on a fine color and polish with time and friction. An almost equivalent substitute is English ash, but this is prone to splinter and cannot be friction-polished at all.

We have already seen, in Chapter II, examples of these "turn-eyed" chairs of seventeenth century date, and we know that these copy, in turn, others from the sixteenth which have disappeared in the natural course of time. The striking difference between the chairs of the seventeenth and those of the eighteenth centuries is that every detail is produced on the lathe, the seat alone excepted, whereas the later chairs owe the back, central splat when present, the seat and the arms to the chair-maker or the carver.

With a type as fixed as this, one would expect a high stage of development, and that is exactly what we find. These chairs are cheap to produce (which means that they are used and appreciated by a great many people) ; they are exceedingly comfortable (which the seventeenth century types are not, as a rule) ; they are durable, easily repaired, and do not require the adventitious aid of upholstery to make them satisfactory.

GREATEST DEVELOPMENT OF THE WINDSOR IN AMERICA

THE Windsor (to give it the English name) with its ease of production, durable and inexpensive character, is *par excellence,* the chair for the new settlement, and in America it develops to a far greater degree than in England. The chair with the right arm end enlarged into a pear-shaped shelf for writing, and with a drawer under the seat to contain paper, is unknown in England. Others appear to have been designed, with dipped top rails to the backs, to serve as barbers' chairs, and the ingenuity shown in some of these models is amazing. It is unnecessary here to illustrate any of the English Windsors; they are fully represented in the American models.

The seat of the Windsor, whether American or English, is invariably hollowed out into a "saddle" form, and it is only when one attempts to re-design the "dishing" in a novel way that the tradition which lies behind the form is appreciated. The backs are generally of two kinds: the bow, where the shaping is one unbroken sweep from the seat-rail upwards, and the "comb-back" where the cresting rail is distinct and undulating and the upright balusters or "lists" have the appearance of acting as the teeth to a comb, hence the name.

STYLES RELATED TO THE WINDSOR

THERE is another variety of chair which owes as much to the turner as to the chair-maker, and which is typically American, that is the so-called "waggon chair," a name probably derived from the use to which they were put, as emergency seats on farm wagons. They are usually coarse, and with little or no lathe-detail or members in the turning. Among this kind is the "ladder-back," a form derived not from the Chippendale, as one would suppose, but from the English James II tall-back chairs where these "ladder-rungs" were first introduced.

The so-called "bobbin-turning" which one finds so much in evidence in the English Commonwealth chairs and tables (and which one would expect to find among the Puritan settlers of New England) and of which one American example is shown here, is really an off-shoot from these "turneyed" chairs, which as we have seen, have so venerable a pedigree, extending from the sixteenth century right down to the present day.

REINFORCING "LISTS" AT BACK. RUSH SEAT

ARM CHAIR IN HICKORY, ELM AND ASH

REINFORCING "LISTS" AT BACK. RUSH SEAT

ROCKER IN HICKORY, ELM AND ASH

AMERICAN BOW-BACK WINDSOR CHAIRS

GOTHIC CHIPPENDALE SUGGESTION IN POINTED BOW AND PIERCED SPLAT

MADE IN HICKORY, ASH AND ELM

SIMPLE TYPE IN HICKORY, ELM AND YEW

ROCKER IN HICKORY, ASH AND ELM

AMERICAN BOW-BACK WINDSOR CHAIRS

HICKORY AND ELM, LAST HALF *18*TH CENTURY

HICKORY, ASH AND ELM, *c. 1770*

WITH BARBER'S EXTENSION TO BACK, *c. 1770*

WRITING CHAIR WITH WRITING ARM, PAPER BOX AND DRAWER, LATE *18*TH CENTURY

AMERICAN COMB-BACK WINDSOR CHAIRS

RARE, PAINTED AMERICAN WINDSOR CHAIR, *c. 1750.* COMB-BACK, TOP RAIL WITH SCROLLED ENDS, ARMS BROADER AT ENDS AND SUPPORTED BY UNUSUAL BALUSTERS, EXTRA WIDE SADDLE SEAT

AMERICAN COMB-BACK WINDSOR CHAIR

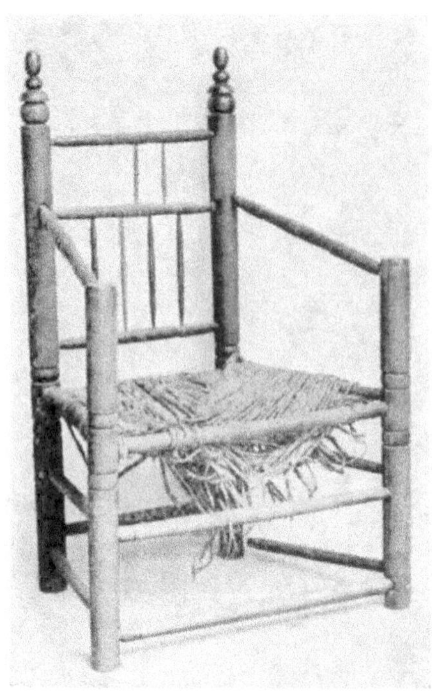

IN ASH AND MAPLE, *c. 1700*

IN HICKORY AND ASH, *c. 1720*

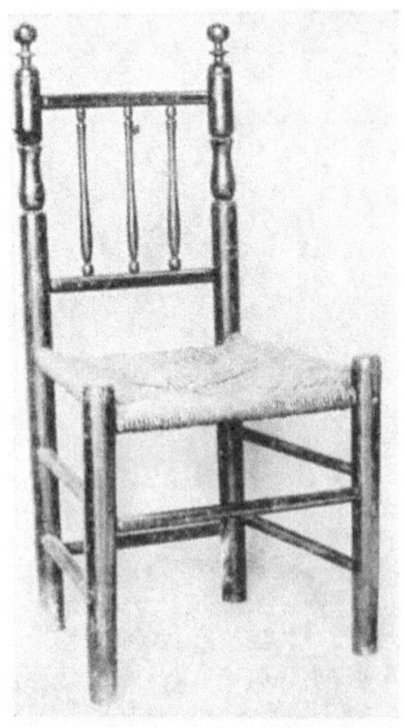

IN ASH AND MAPLE, *c. 1700*

IN HICKORY AND MAPLE, LATE *17*TH CENTURY

AMERICAN TURNED CHAIRS OF WINDSOR TYPE

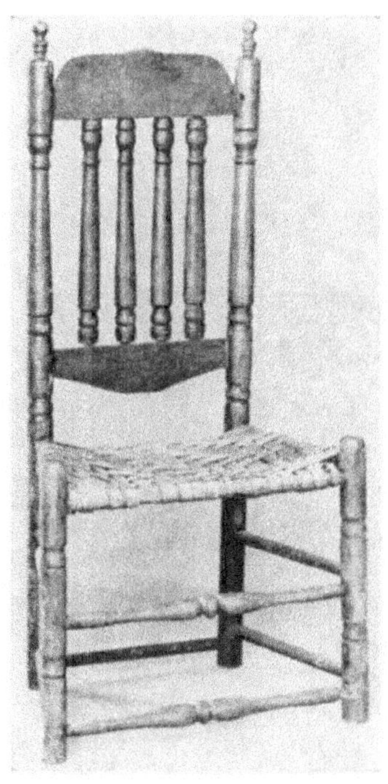

HICKORY AND MAPLE, EARLY *18*TH CENTURY

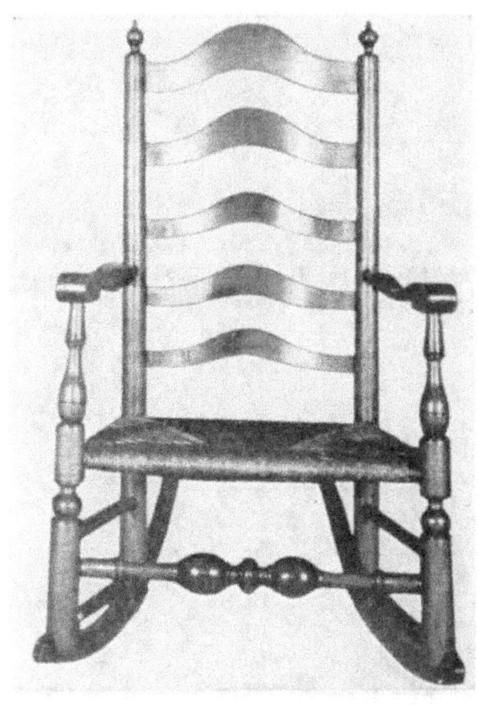

LADDER-BACK ROCKER IN MAPLE AND CHERRY, NEW ENGLAND, *c. 1730*

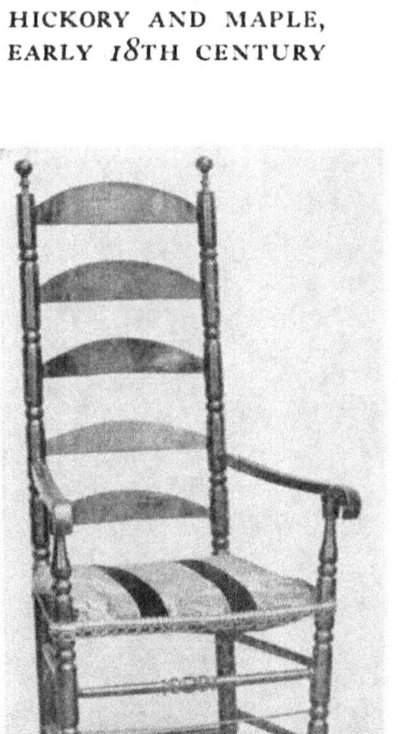

TALL LADDER-BACK OF LATE *17*TH CENTURY, ENGLISH MODEL

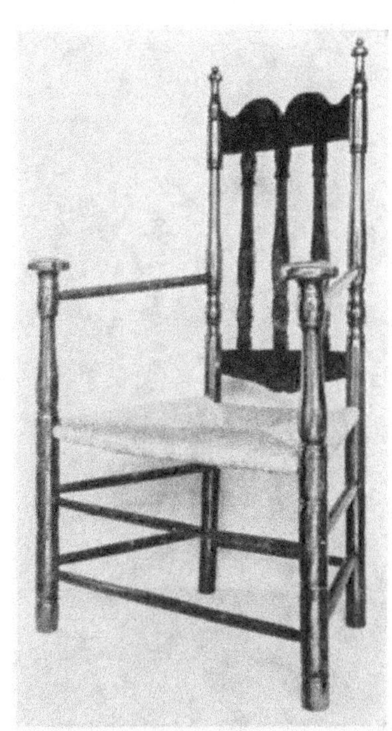

HICKORY AND MAPLE WITH RUSH SEAT, FIRST HALF *18*TH CENTURY

AMERICAN TURNED CHAIRS OF WINDSOR TYPE

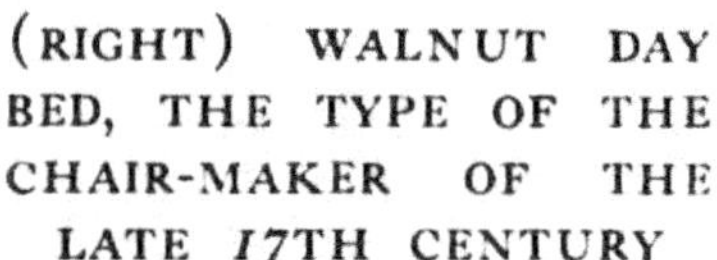
(RIGHT) WALNUT DAY BED, THE TYPE OF THE CHAIR-MAKER OF THE LATE *17*TH CENTURY

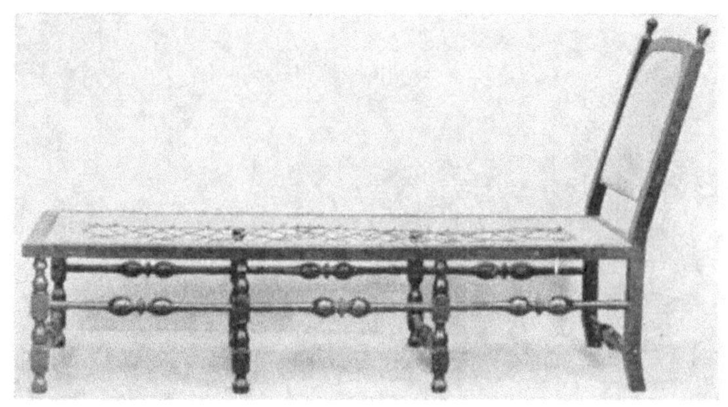

(LEFT) MAPLE DAY BED PAINTED RED, NEW ENGLAND DEVELOPMENT FROM WINDSOR OR WAGON CHAIR TYPE. MID *18*TH CENTURY

(LEFT) "BOBBIN" TURNED CHAIR IN MAPLE, LAST QUARTER *17*TH CENTURY

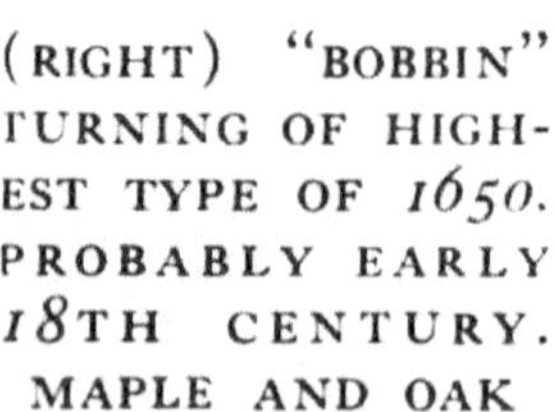
(RIGHT) "BOBBIN" TURNING OF HIGHEST TYPE OF *1650*. PROBABLY EARLY *18*TH CENTURY. MAPLE AND OAK

AMERICAN TURNED FURNITURE DEVELOPED FROM THE WINDSOR CHAIR

CHAPTER V

LACQUER WORK

AMERICAN LACQUER VERY RARE

IT IS unnecessary to treat of American lacquer work in any detail. It was, at best, purely an adventitious decoration, and was very sparingly used. The dry climate of the Eastern American states, the rigors of a New England winter, with the consequent tendency to overheat the houses, must have been fatal to its popularity here. At the present day it is dangerous to introduce the English pieces which, in a humid climate, have persisted in a perfect state for nearly three hundred years. In America the best European examples fall to pieces in an incredibly short time. The same is true of the Chinese work, which one would have thought could withstand any extremes of temperature. American lacquered pieces are exceedingly rare, in consequence, and, in inspiration and design, are far removed from oriental originals.

LACQUER WORK IN ENGLAND

IN ENGLAND, in the years from 1660 to about 1730, attempts were made to design furniture specifically for lacquer ornamentation, and in the closing years of the seventeenth century, a definite fashion for lacquer did exist, shared, perhaps with the craze for marqueterie, an inlay of gaily colored woods. From these years we get the square cabinets on carved gilt stands, ornate pieces which may have suited the large architectural interiors of the time, but which would have been sadly out of place in a New England settler's home.

Lacquer persists, in England, throughout the period of the Chippendale school, and Robert Adam used it at Nostell Priory and at Gawthorp (afterwards Harewood House). It appears, sporadically, even up to the end of the century, in the work of Hepplewhite and Sheraton, but this late lacquer is really varnished paint, and differs, intrinsically, very little, if at all, from the decoration of Pergolesi, Antonio Zucchi, Cipriani or Angelica Kauffmann, other than in style. Various attempts were made to revive this "Chinese taste," as it was termed. Edwards and Darly in 1745, Chippendale in 1754–62, and even Sheraton in 1795 designed in this manner, and the last named even devised a chair-pattern in wood turned to simulate bamboo, and intended for lacquering in brown with Chinese devices picked out in gold. At the same time a rage did exist for Chinese wall-papers (of which numbers were imported in the "tea-clippers") and fabrics in the oriental styles. As early as 1688 Stalker and Parker had published a folio volume in which they proposed to teach the whole art and mystery of "lackering" or "Japanning," but they were merely charlatans, as a study of the book (now very rare, by the way) will show.

SQUARE CABINET DECORATED WITH BLACK LACQUER ON CARVED AND GILT STAND, AND WITH PEDIMENT TO MATCH. CHASED BRASS HINGES AND LOCK PLATE, *c. 1670*

ENGLISH LACQUER CABINET

GREEN LACQUER SQUARE CABINET ON CARVED AND GILT STAND. ENGRAVED AND GILT BRASS CORNER HINGES AND LOCK PLATE. A COPY FROM THE FRENCH LOUIS XIV, *c. 1720*

ENGLISH LACQUER CABINET

SQUARE BLACK LACQUER CABINET ON CARVED GILT STAND.
EARLY GEORGIAN STYLE, *c. 1725–30*

ENGLISH LACQUER CABINET

DOUBLE-DOMED CABINET ON STAND, BLACK LACQUER, *c. 1690*

ENGLISH LACQUER CABINET

(LEFT) CORNER CABINET. BLACK LACQUER, CHINESE. EARLY *18*TH CENTURY, ENGLISH

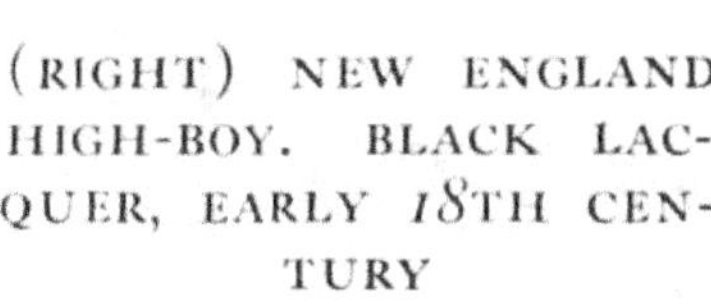

(RIGHT) NEW ENGLAND HIGH-BOY. BLACK LACQUER, EARLY *18*TH CENTURY

(LEFT) SQUARE CABINET IN CHIPPENDALE STYLE, FRETTED STAND. BLACK LACQUER, ENGLISH

(RIGHT) NEW ENGLAND MAPLE CHEST ON STAND. LACQUER DECORATION ON BARE WOOD. EARLY *18*TH CENTURY

ENGLISH AND AMERICAN LACQUER CABINETS AND CHESTS

COMMODE IN BLACK AND GOLD LACQUER MADE BY CHIPPENDALE, HAIG & COMPANY FOR THE EARL OF DUNDONALD AND PROBABLY DESIGNED BY ROBERT ADAM, *c. 1765.* AN EXAMPLE OF LACQUER WORK PERSISTING TO THE LATE *18*TH CENTURY

ENGLISH LACQUER COMMODE

CHAPTER VI

THE DEVELOPMENT OF THE ENGLISH WALNUT CHAIR

CHANGE IN CHAIR DESIGN

THE restoration of the monarchy, in 1660, witnesses the birth of a distinct trade, that of the chair-maker. A comparison between the oak and the walnut models (the former still persist until almost the close of the seventeenth century) will show totally distinct traditions and methods in each. Foreign influences, from the Low Countries, France, Portugal and Spain, undoubtedly account for much of this, but not for all. New design-motives from abroad, and the use of a new wood, might both effect considerable changes, but not in tradition. The old era of the heavily-made chair had come to an end, and a new race of makers had come to the front.

If chair and furniture making had still been the province of the one trade, we would expect to find the same evolutionary process in both, but at the period when the typical Restoration walnut chair, with its spiral turned balusters, arm supports, legs and stretcher rails, was being made as a novelty, the older heavy court cupboard had not gone out of fashion. It was inevitable that the advantages, from the points of appearance, cost and movability, should be quickly appreciated, and we find this new chair-making trade turning its attention to tables and similar pieces, and even to wall furniture such as cabinets and escritoires.

With walnut, also, comes the age of veneering (which, in itself, involves a tremendous modification of method) and this develops again into the era of marqueterie. It is with the chairs of the period from 1660 to about 1725 that the most rapid evolution takes place, which fact, in itself, suggests that the trade was new and receptive to fresh impressions. The Early Restoration chair, intrinsically, constitutes a considerable departure from the older—and still persisting—oak models.

The change really begins in the latter days of the Commonwealth, with the introduction of the slide-rest as an adjunct to the lathe, which renders spiral turning easy, exact and practical. Thus, we get, with this new tool, a partial reversion to the older "turneyed" chair of the sixteenth and seventeenth centuries. These turned chairs of the Cromwellian period have their counterparts in the early productions of New England, which one would expect, considering the rationality of the new settlers. For the same reasons, or on account of religious prejudices, the Restoration models were rarely copied, but a revulsion took place before the race of the Stuarts came to an end in 1689 (with the flight of the last of that unstable and treacherous family to the Court of Saint Germain) as the tall-back chairs of 1685–9 are freely copied in Massachusetts and Rhode Island.

CHARACTERISTICS OF RESTORATION CHAIRS

THE first Restoration models are lightly, but soundly constructed. Between the twisted balusters of the back, the cresting rail (often carved with the royal crown) is tenoned, and even the squares of the front legs are taken up beyond the seat, the framing of the latter being notched between them. The legs, in addition, are firmly tied with cross rails, and in the first models, a front stretcher, pierced and carved, is introduced between the front legs, just below the seat-framing. It is curious, and instructive, to trace the evolutionary change through which this stretcher rapidly passes. In a few years it is placed lower down, then tenoned between the cross railing instead of the legs, then is made in the form of a crested X, tying all four legs together, and, in the first years of William III it becomes flat, and in serpentine shape, but still retaining its X form. It then disappears entirely, being replaced, for a time, by the older form of turned cross railing, until in the first mahogany years, the legs of chairs cease to be tied together in any way, but stand free. Anticipating, for a moment, a later chapter in this book, the cross railing is again revived by Chippendale, in his square-leg models, and by Hepplewhite.

The first notable change in the legs of these early walnut chairs is the introduction of the Flemish curve and double C scroll for the shaping of the legs. The next is the fashion for abnormally tall backs—a short-lived one, by the way, as it must have been discovered that these chairs had a marked tendency to overbalance and to fall backwards. The next modification in construction (and a bad one) was to dowel the cresting rails of the backs on to the outer balusters, instead of tenoning them between the squares, as with the early Restoration examples. At the same period, the seat frames were simply pegged to the front legs, a weak method which, luckily, was not possible in the case of an armchair, where the front legs had to be prolonged to act as arm supports with the seat fixed between them.

The Flemish curve tends to disappear in the early Orange years, after 1690, being replaced by turning, beginning with the Portuguese bulb, which, in turn, rapidly develops into the inverted cup, a detail borrowed from Holland. At the same time the whorled Spanish, (or Braganza) foot changes to the flattened "bun" form, the latter being extensively used for cabinets and tables. In these early Orange years, also, the fashion begins for making the backs of chairs either as a complete frame, solid upholstered or carved, or with several pierced and carved splats connecting the top rail with the back of the seat. At the same time there is another form, borrowed from France, where the back panel is entirely filled with pierced and carved ornament, in the designing of which the influence of the Louis XIV style is very evident.

DESIGN CHANGES ABOUT 1700

THE dawn of the eighteenth century witnesses a radical change in chairs. The smooth cabriole leg is introduced in its perfect form. It had been used, in an embryonic, and disconnected form, some years before, but the perfectly smooth cabriole belongs to the first years of the reign of Anne. With it goes the smooth hoop-back, where the top rail continues down to the seat-frame in an unbroken line. The arms of chairs and settees follow the same fashion. In these early hoop-back chairs, there is generally one shaped broad central splat, which is nearly always veneered with burr or finely figured walnut. It is the first time that veneering is introduced into English chair construction.

Judging from the extreme rarity of marqueterie inlay in chairs, the fashion must have left the chair-maker comparatively unaffected. another proof that he worked on distinct lines as compared with the maker of other furniture. Lacquered chairs are more plentiful, but far from being general. Throughout the later seventeenth and the first half of the eighteenth centuries the same evolutionary factors never appear to govern chairs and wall furniture at the same time or in the same way.

In the first years of George I changes in chair-forms also proceed with bewildering rapidity, but there are no influences from Germany apparent (unless it be in the sole instance of the lion furniture) which one might have expected with the accession of the first of the House of Brunswick. The older hoop-back still persists, but begins to be more elaborated. I have styled this early Georgian period, in another book*, the decorated Queen Anne, for want of a better name. We get the lion or satyr mask, and the lion's paw, and the eagle's head is also found in many of these later walnut examples.

INTRODUCTION OF MAHOGANY

MAHOGANY comes into general use shortly after 1725, but changes in furniture, and especially in chair-types, are not as pronounced as one would have expected. True, we get again a reversion to the older solid construction, without veneering, but this does not persist for long, the introduction of the finely figured woods bringing the veneering press, the caul and the hammer again into use. The lion period, from about 1730 to 1740, is more of a mahogany than a walnut style, but examples can be found in both woods. This manner, in turn, is supplanted by the "cabochon-and-leaf" ornament, in conjunction either with the earlier ball-and-claw, or the leaf-carved foot, and the next progression, in its order, carries us into the manner of the Chippendale school.

It is posterity alone which has segregated all these various manners into distinct styles. Actually, the progression from the one to the other is gradual, and rarely, if ever, continuous. Thus we get late features and earlier details in the one piece, as an examination of the examples illustrated in this chapter will show. At no period in the whole of the history of English furniture were fashions so arbitrary that earlier motives did not persist. The same details, used at different periods, do vary, however, in a certain minute measure, but it requires the trained eye of the expert to detect the distinction.

*English Furniture of the Eighteenth Century.

In conclusion, it must be borne in mind that anyone can revert, but no one can anticipate, therefore it is the latest detail which is the true guide in estimating the date of any particular piece. This ignores the wide subject of later copying, or actual forgery, but this again is the field of the expert, and is utterly beyond the scope of this, or any other book.

ARMCHAIR, *c. 1660.* BOBBIN REPLACED BY SPIRAL TURNING IN LAST YEARS OF COMMONWEALTH. REALLY A PERSISTENCE OF THE TUDOR "TURNEYED" CHAIR

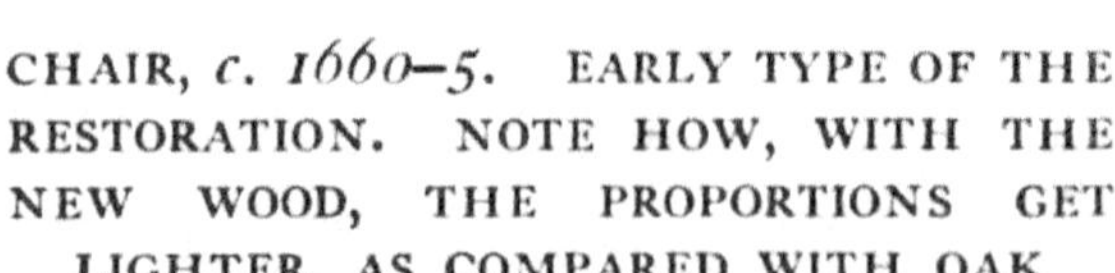

CHAIR, *c. 1660–5.* EARLY TYPE OF THE RESTORATION. NOTE HOW, WITH THE NEW WOOD, THE PROPORTIONS GET LIGHTER, AS COMPARED WITH OAK

DEVELOPMENT OF ENGLISH WALNUT CHAIRS FROM 1660 TO 1700

ARMCHAIR, *c. 1660–70.* INTRODUCTION OF CANED PANEL IN BACK AND SEAT. USUALLY PROVIDED WITH VELVET SQUAB CUSHION, TIED BY CORDS AT CORNERS

ARMCHAIR, *c. 1660–70.* NOTE CONSTRUCTION; CRESTING RAIL OF BACK IN THESE EARLY MODELS IS TENONED BETWEEN SIDE BALUSTERS. LATER IT IS PEGGED ON TOP

DEVELOPMENT OF ENGLISH WALNUT CHAIRS FROM 1660 TO 1700

ARMCHAIR, *c. 1660–70.* VELVET SQUAB CUSHION TIED AT THE CORNERS WITH CORD AND TASSELS. THE ORIGINAL CANING OF THE BACK HAS BEEN REPLACED BY UPHOLSTERY

ARMCHAIR, *c. 1660.* THE EARLIEST TYPE, THE LEGS CARRIED TO THE FLOOR WITH SQUARES, WITHOUT TURNED FEET. NO CARVED STRETCHER BETWEEN THE FRONT LEGS, ONLY A TWISTED RAIL

DEVELOPMENT OF ENGLISH WALNUT CHAIRS FROM 1660 TO 1700

ARMCHAIR, *c. 1680–5.* ELABORATE TYPE OF THE LATER RESTORATION YEARS, WITH THE INTRODUCTION OF THE FLEMISH SCROLL IN THE FRONT LEGS, ARM SUPPORTS AND FRONT STRETCHER. THE CRESTING RAIL IS STILL TENONED BETWEEN THE SIDE BALUSTERS

DEVELOPMENT OF ENGLISH WALNUT CHAIRS FROM 1660 TO 1700

ARMCHAIR, *c. 1685.* THE FULL DEVELOPMENT OF THE FLEMISH CURVE OR DOUBLE C-SCROLL, IMMEDIATELY PRECEDING THE ERA OF THE HIGH BACK IN ENGLISH CHAIRS (SEE LATER). NOTE THE LIGHTER CONSTRUCTION OF THE BACK

DEVELOPMENT OF ENGLISH WALNUT CHAIRS FROM 1660 TO 1700

ARMCHAIR, *c. 1685.* THE RESTORATION CONSTRUCTION, BUT THE FLEMISH CURVE USED EVERYWHERE

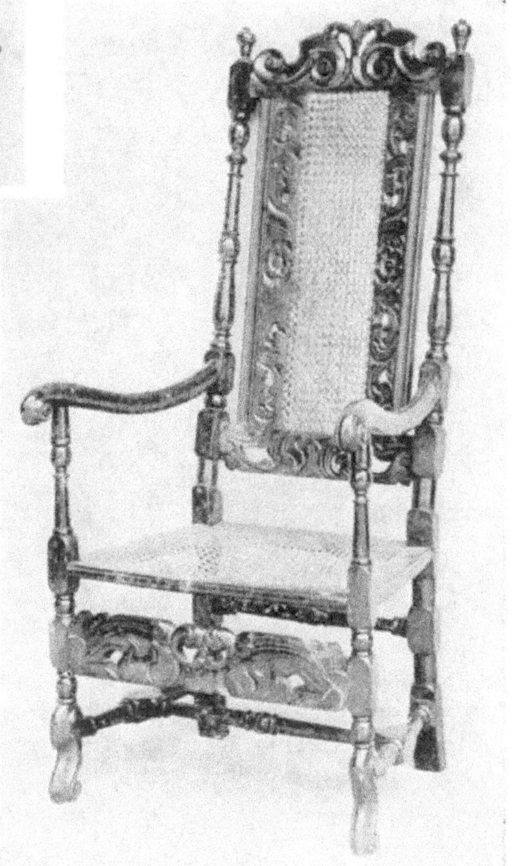

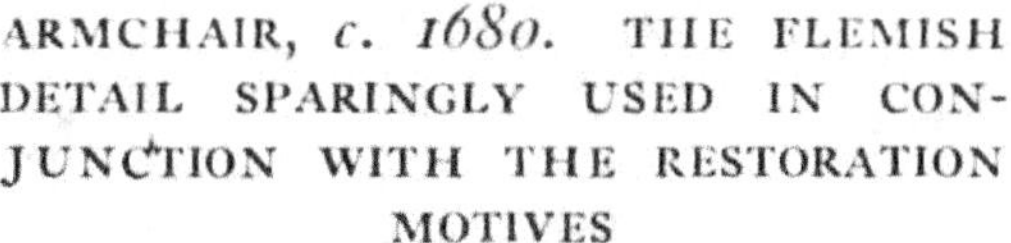

ARMCHAIR, *c. 1680.* THE FLEMISH DETAIL SPARINGLY USED IN CONJUNCTION WITH THE RESTORATION MOTIVES

DEVELOPMENT OF ENGLISH WALNUT CHAIRS FROM 1660 TO 1700

(LEFT) ARMCHAIR, *c. 1685.* LOW COUNTRY DETAILS INTRODUCED IN AN ELABORATE MODEL. A RARE EXAMPLE WITH LIONS' HEADS ON ARMS

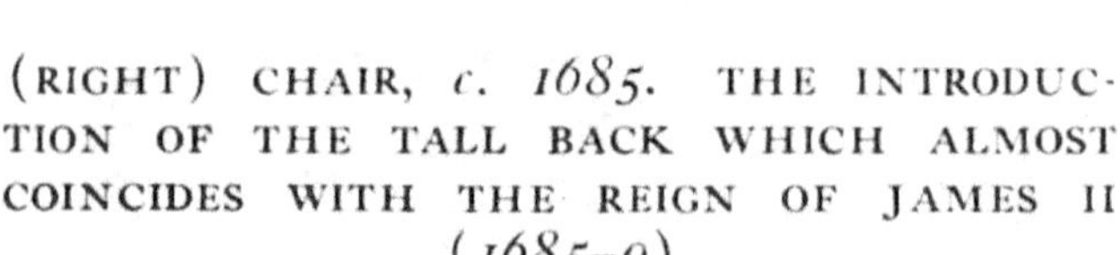

(RIGHT) CHAIR, *c. 1685.* THE INTRODUCTION OF THE TALL BACK WHICH ALMOST COINCIDES WITH THE REIGN OF JAMES II (*1685–9*)

DEVELOPMENT OF ENGLISH WALNUT CHAIRS FROM 1660 TO 1700

SETTEE COVERED WITH NEEDLEPOINT. TYPE OF ENGLISH STYLE OF *1680–5*. EARLY DETAILS ARE INTRODUCED IN THE CARVED STRETCHERS WHERE THE CROWN FLANKED BY AMORINI AND SCROLLWORK UNITE THE FRONT LEGS. THE LATTER ARE OF FLEMISH TYPE

DEVELOPMENT OF ENGLISH WALNUT CHAIRS FROM 1660 TO 1700

WALNUT SETTEE COVERED WITH NEEDLEPOINT, *c. 1685.* FLEMISH TYPE OF LEGS AND STRETCHERS

DEVELOPMENT OF ENGLISH WALNUT CHAIRS FROM 1660 TO 1700

CHAIRS OF THIS KIND WERE MADE WITH ADJUSTABLE BACKS, FOR USE AS "SLEEPING CHAIRS." EXAMPLES EXIST AT HAM HOUSE, PETERSHAM. *c. 1685*

DEVELOPMENT OF ENGLISH WALNUT CHAIRS FROM 1660 TO 1700

ARMCHAIRS, *c. 1685*. STATE CHAIRS OF THIS KIND WERE MADE FOR IMPORTANT ROOMS, COVERED IN VELVET, NEEDLEPOINT OR TAPESTRY. THREE NOTABLE EXAMPLES

DEVELOPMENT OF ENGLISH WALNUT CHAIRS FROM 1660 TO 1700

BEECH CHAIR, *c. 1685.* THE TALL BACK WITH THE LATER CONSTRUCTION WHERE THE TOP RAIL IS PEGGED ON TO THE SIDE BALUSTERS OF THE BACK, NOT TENONED BETWEEN THEM

BEECH ARMCHAIR, *c. 1685.* CHAIRS OF THIS KIND ARE THE PROTOTYPES OF SOME OF THE NEW ENGLAND MODELS OF *1700*

WALNUT CHAIR, *c. 1685–90.* FLEMISH CURVES IN BACK, LEGS AND STRETCHER, AND TRIPLE SPLATS

WALNUT CHAIR, *1685–90.* INTRODUCING NEW DETAILS OF THE TRIPLE PIERCED AND CARVED SPLATS IN THE BACKS, AND THE FLATTENED X STRETCHER BETWEEN THE LEGS

DEVELOPMENT OF ENGLISH WALNUT CHAIRS FROM 1660 TO 1700

CHAIR, *c. 1690.* TALL BACK IN ONE PANEL, CANED, CUP-TURNED LEGS IN THE ORANGE STYLE. FLEMISH FRONT STRETCHER

THE LAST PHASE OF THE TALL-BACK CHAIR, BACK IN ONE CANED PANEL. FLEMISH TYPE OF LEGS AND STRETCHER. *c. 1690*

DEVELOPMENT OF ENGLISH WALNUT CHAIRS FROM 1660 TO 1700

ARMCHAIRS, *c. 1695*. THE FRAMED AND CANED BACK, CUP-TURNED LEGS AND FLAT SERPENTINE OR X STRETCHER

CHAIRS, *c. 1690–5*. SIMILAR TO THE ABOVE, AND INTRODUCING DETAILS FROM HOLLAND

DEVELOPMENT OF ENGLISH WALNUT CHAIRS FROM 1660 TO 1700

CHAIRS, *c. 1690.* ENGLISH AND LOUIS XIV INFLUENCES. NOTE THE POSITION OF THE CRESTED STRETCHERS, WHICH ARE NOW FIXED BETWEEN THE CROSS RAILS INSTEAD OF THE FRONT LEGS

CHAIR, *c. 1690.* THE FRAMED AND CARVED ORANGE BACK WITH JAMES II DETAILS PERSISTING

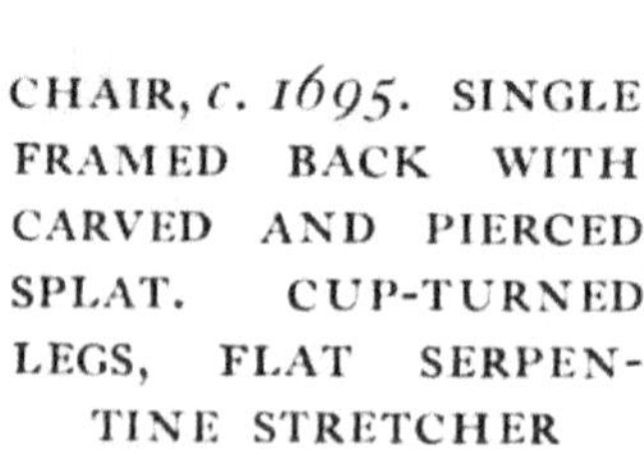

CHAIR, *c. 1695.* SINGLE FRAMED BACK WITH CARVED AND PIERCED SPLAT. CUP-TURNED LEGS, FLAT SERPENTINE STRETCHER

DEVELOPMENT OF ENGLISH WALNUT CHAIRS FROM 1660 TO 1700

ARMCHAIR, *c. 1695*. THE ELABORATE TYPE OF THIS PERIOD, WITH CARVED CRESTING RAIL DOWELLED ON TOP OF THE SIDE BALUSTERS, TRIPLE CARVED SPLAT, TURNED FRONT LEGS WITH "BUN" FEET, AND FLAT STRETCHER. NOTE THE APPLIED MOULDING ROUND THE SEAT RAIL

DEVELOPMENT OF ENGLISH WALNUT CHAIRS FROM 1660 TO 1700

WING EASY CHAIR, *c. 1695.* FRONT LEGS TURNED WITH THE PORTUGUESE AND SPANISH WHORLED FEET. COVERED WITH PETIT-POINT NEEDLEWORK REPRESENTING SUSANNAH AND THE ELDERS AND OTHER BIBLICAL STORIES. THE WING CHAIR IS RARE AT THIS DATE

DEVELOPMENT OF ENGLISH WALNUT CHAIRS FROM 1660 TO 1700

BEECH GILT ARMCHAIR, *c. 1695–1700.* A LITERAL COPY FROM THE LOUIS XIV. COVERED WITH ENGLISH NEEDLEWORK OF CONTEMPORARY DATE IN DROP STITCH

DEVELOPMENT OF ENGLISH WALNUT CHAIRS FROM 1660 TO 1700

BEECH, BLACK PAINTED SETTEE COVERED WITH PETIT-POINT NEEDLE-WORK, *c. 1700–5*. INTRODUCTION OF THE SMOOTH CABRIOLE LEG

DEVELOPMENT OF ENGLISH WALNUT CHAIRS FROM 1660 TO 1700

WING CHAIR. THE SMOOTH CABRIOLE LEG WITH CLUB FOOT OF THE EARLY EXAMPLES OF *c. 1705*

DEVELOPMENT OF ENGLISH WALNUT CHAIRS FROM 1660 TO 1700

ARMCHAIR, ENGLISH, *c. 1710.* HOOP BACK WITH INSET PANEL TO ACCOMMODATE NEEDLEWORK (A DETAIL RARE IN FURNITURE OF THIS DATE). ARMS CURVED TO SEAT IN ONE UNBROKEN LINE. CABRIOLE LEGS BEGIN TO BE DECORATED, SHOWING LATER PHASE OF QUEEN ANNE STYLE

DEVELOPMENT OF ENGLISH WALNUT CHAIRS FROM 1660 TO 1700

CHAIR-BACK SETTEE, *c. 1710.* THE BROAD CENTRAL SPLATS ARE PIERCED AND CARVED. THE ARMS SWEEP DOWN FROM BALUSTER TO SEAT IN ONE UNBROKEN LINE. THE CABRIOLE LEGS NOW CREST UP OVER THE SEAT RAIL INSTEAD OF FINISHING BENEATH IT

DEVELOPMENT OF ENGLISH WALNUT CHAIRS FROM 1660 TO 1700

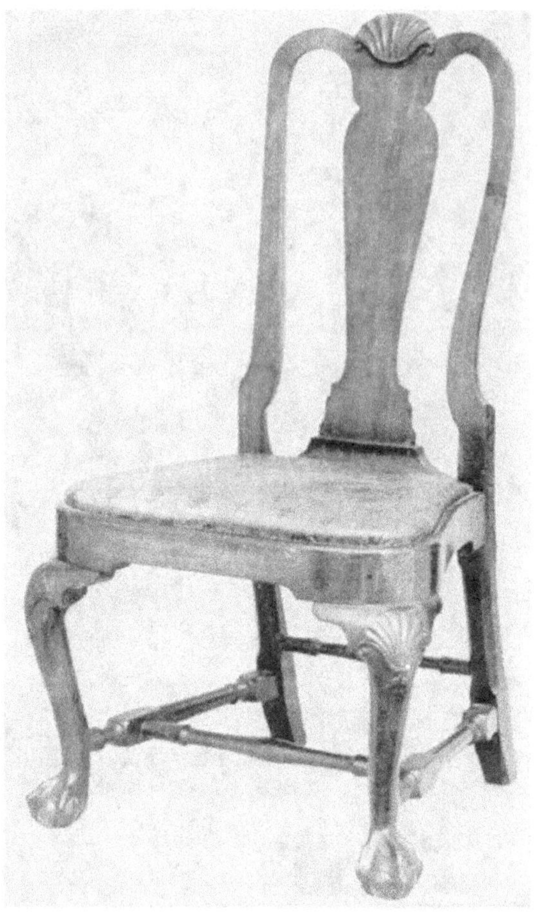

WALNUT CHAIR, C. *1705*. THE EARLY TYPE WHERE THE LEGS ARE STILL TIED WITH TURNED STRETCHER RAILS

MAHOGANY CHAIR, *c. 1735*. ELABORATE EARLY GEORGIAN TYPE INTRODUCING LION'S MASK AND PAW. A CHAIR OF THIS DESIGN IS IN SIR JOHN SOANE'S MUSEUM IN LINCOLN'S INN FIELDS

ENGLISH CHAIRS, THE COMMENCEMENT OF MAHOGANY, IN THE LION YEARS, c. 1735

BEECH GILT AND GESSO SETTEE, *c. 1735.* THE HOOP BACK STILL RETAINED, BUT WITH THE LATER TYPE OF ARM. CABRIOLE LEGS WITH LION MASKS AND PAW FEET

WALNUT CHAIRS, *c. 1735.* HOOP BACKS AND LION-CARVED CABRIOLE LEGS. AN EXAMPLE OF HOW WALNUT PERSISTS INTO THE MAHOGANY YEARS

ENGLISH CHAIRS OF THE LION YEARS, c. 1735

WALNUT WING CHAIR, *c. 1735*. COVERED WITH PETIT-POINT NEEDLEWORK IN SILK AND WOOL. THE PAW FEET INDICATE THE MAHOGANY YEARS

ENGLISH CHAIR OF THE EARLY MAHOGANY PERIOD

WRITING CHAIR COVERED WITH NEEDLEWORK, *c. 1735–40*. THE DEVELOPMENT TOWARDS THE CHIPPENDALE

ENGLISH CHAIR OF THE EARLY MAHOGANY PERIOD

CHAPTER VII

ENGLISH AND AMERICAN MAHOGANY CHAIRS

EARLY GEORGIAN TO CHIPPENDALE

WALNUT AND MAHOGANY OVERLAP

WHILE the transition from oak to walnut in English furniture involves a somewhat drastic change in design, and especially in proportion, the same is not true where mahogany begins to replace walnut, shortly after 1725. As we have seen, in both text and illustration, in the previous chapter, types merge the one into the other, irrespective of wood; in fact, the examples in both timbers actually overlap, the use of the one or the other being optional, in the early years, perhaps dictated by conditions, such as the stocks of walnut or mahogany available at certain times and in different localities. This is true, to a far greater degree, of chairs than of other furniture, as veneering enters into the field of the latter to a far greater degree than of the former, with the hiatus from 1725 to about 1735, when mahogany was used, in the older solid fashion, for both.

CLASSIFYING STYLES

CHAIRS from 1725 onward, pursuing the even continuity of development from the Queen Anne right up to the close of the Chippendale period (nearly to 1780) may be resolved into certain subclasses thus:

(1) The hoop-back, the Queen Anne form persisting.

(2) The pierced back or central splat, this piercing taking the forms of plain vertical divisions, or an elaborate interlacing, in which a representation of the figure 8 largely predominates.

(3) The use of the "paper-scroll," especially in the junctions of the top rail of the back with the side balusters.

(4) The use of the vase-shaped central splat, either solid or pierced in simple fashion.

(5) The lion-mask, on the knees of cabriole legs and on the ends of arms, usually in conjunction with the paw foot.

(6) The cabochon-and-leaf decoration on the knees of cabriole legs.

(7) The wing easy chair which belongs to both the walnut and the mahogany periods, but which is more general in the latter.

(8) The chairs of the Chippendale school, which can again be resolved into classes or styles, thus:

(a) The Gothic.
(b) The square leg, fretted or plain.
(c) The cabriole style.
(d) The French manner.
(e) The Chinese manner.

AS TO CHIPPENDALE

It is not the place here to consider the work or the style of Thomas Chippendale, as this belongs, properly, to a succeeding chapter. It will be sufficient, for the present purpose, to state, briefly, four propositions:

(1) If we admit creation of a definite style by Thomas Chippendale, in his "Gentleman and Cabinetmaker's Director" (1754, 1755, 1762) then this is not one style, but at least four.

(2) The publication of other design books, almost contemporary, and some prior to 1754, in which practically the same style, or series of styles, are illustrated (to say nothing of many of the tradesmen's business cards of the period, which are frequently in the "Chippendale manner," but certainly never were designed by Chippendale himself) preclude any such claim to originality.

(3) If we accept the "Director" as the designing guide, then very little of the furniture generally styled as "Chippendale" bears any resemblance to any of the patterns in that book.

(4) The accredited furniture which Thomas Chippendale actually made is all in a manner foreign to his style (being in that of Robert Adam as a rule) which does not suggest that, in the "Director," he was preaching a new and individual gospel.

I have preferred, therefore, to speak of the work of the Chippendale School of craftsmen, as such undoubtedly existed, but this must not be held to mean that this school made furniture in the "Director" manner. The subdivisions used here are the cabriole, the Gothic, the Chinese and the square leg, which are sufficiently obvious to require no further explanation.

In the chair work of this school, solid construction was almost the invariable rule, the only exception being in the case of the Chinese designs, where the whole of the back panel and often the arm openings, are filled with fretwork. For greater strength, and to obviate shrinkage, this fretwork was frequently laminated, that is, built up in three or five layers, the grain of the wood, in alternate strata running transversely to the other layers. The same constructional device (which is eminently a sound one) was also used for the fretted galleries or stretchers of small center tables, either of the five-leg or the tripod variety.

With this furniture of the Chippendale school we get a reversion to the older fine tradition of good construction in furniture, which was such a feature of the earlier oak, as we have seen in previous chapters.

It has already been stated, and may be repeated here with advantage, that posterity has created styles in English furniture, by a process of arbitrary segregation. Actually, the Chippendale merges into the Hepplewhite, and the Hepplewhite into the Sheraton, almost insensibly, but the consideration of the two latter styles belongs to succeeding chapters in this book.

AMERICAN CHAIRS

A WORD or two as to the chairs of Pennsylvania and New England, in conclusion. It is possible that the "Director" penetrated into these states shortly after it was published; it is certain that many of the designs were known in Philadelphia as early as 1770. The patterns of the Chippendale chairs were copied in the Quaker City, but there is one peculiar feature which distinguishes the American from the English chair, almost invariably, that is, the stump form of back leg. This is not an economy in manufacture, as these stump cylindrical legs are, actually, more costly to make than those of the English chairs. It is a fashion borrowed from the Queen Anne walnut models from the Midland Counties. The American term "side chair" is the correct one. The place of the dining room chair, when not in use, was against the side wall of the room, in which position the back legs would not be markedly noticeable. When placed up to the table, it is only the servants who would see the back view of the chairs, and they did not matter. The back of the chair was, therefore, left plain, (not to say ugly) of a deliberate purpose. It was a tradition of the time, in America, especially in the states where negro help was the rule. A similar idea has pertained in all periods, one which is seldom remarked. A chair is the only piece of furniture which is intended to be viewed from all sides, but where the back is left plain of deliberate purpose. A Chippendale chair is never carved at the back, nor is a walnut chair veneered. If the covering of the front be of silk, velvet or needlepoint, then a simple and inexpensive material is invariably selected for the outside back. This is one of the little details which is never noticed—perhaps because it is so obvious.

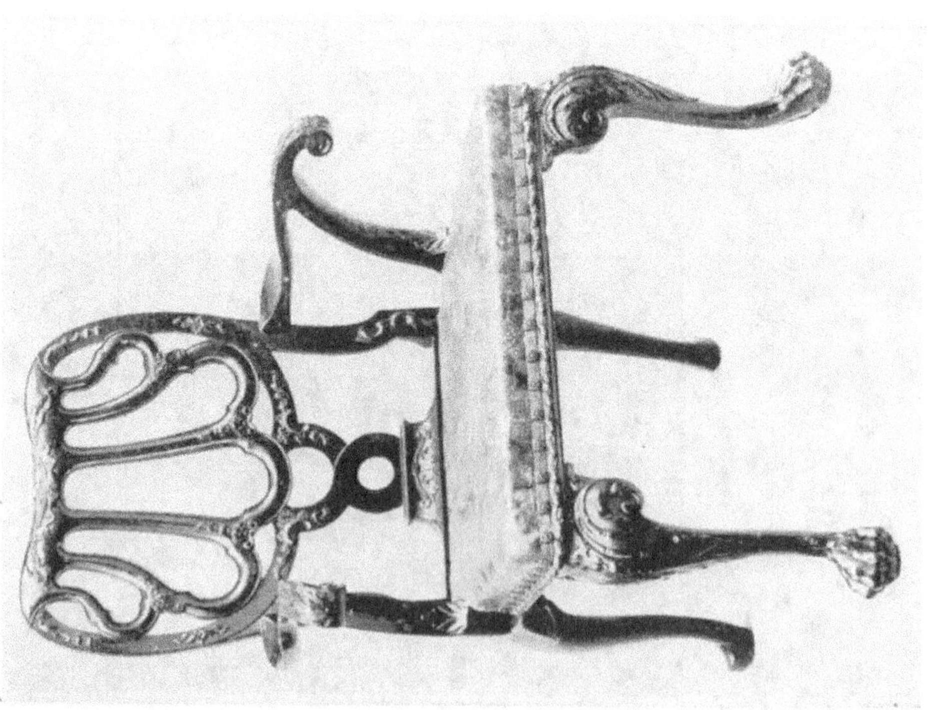

ARM CHAIR, ENGLISH, *c. 1735–40*. THE HOOP-BACK WITH PANEL ENTIRELY FILLED WITH TRACERY. PAW FEET

WRITING CHAIR, ENGLISH, *c. 1735*. COVERED WITH CREWEL WORK. THE EARLY WALNUT TYPE PERSISTING

CABRIOLE CHAIRS OF THE EARLY MAHOGANY PERIOD

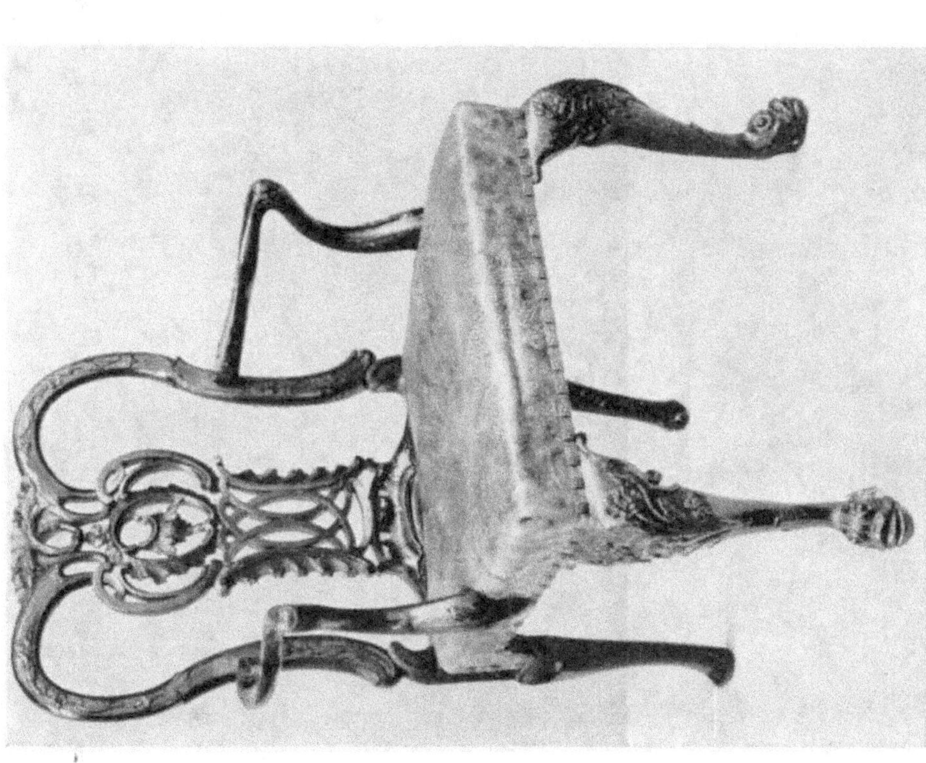

ARM CHAIR, ENGLISH, *c. 1740.* THE HOOP-BACK WITH ELABORATE CENTRAL SPLAT. EARLY TYPE OF ARM, DOLPHIN FEET

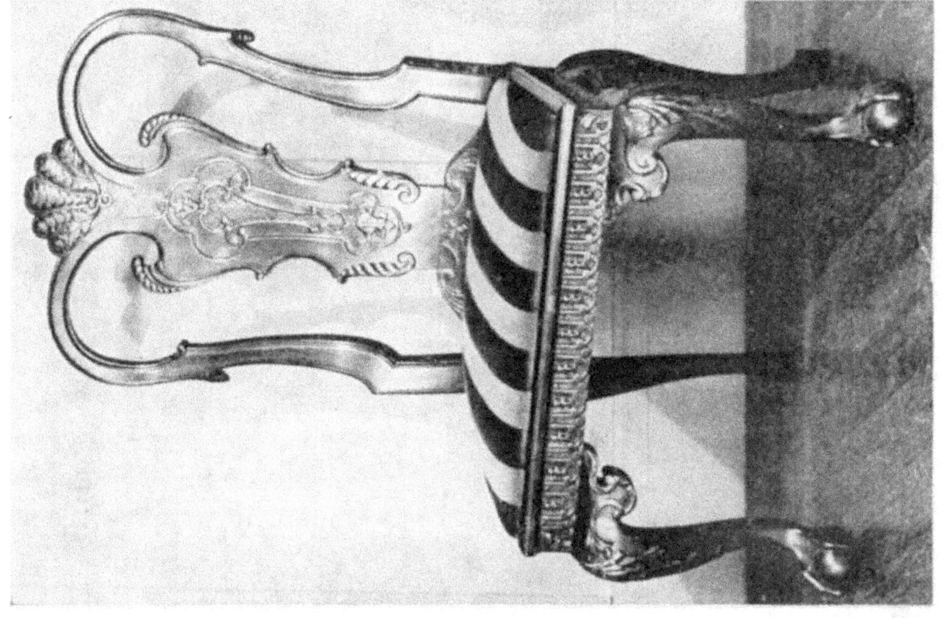

WALNUT CHAIR, ENGLISH TYPE OF *c. 1730.* THE HOOP-BACK IN THE EARLY MAHOGANY YEARS, WITH FRONT LEGS IN THE FASHION OF *c. 1720*

CABRIOLE CHAIRS OF THE EARLY MAHOGANY PERIOD

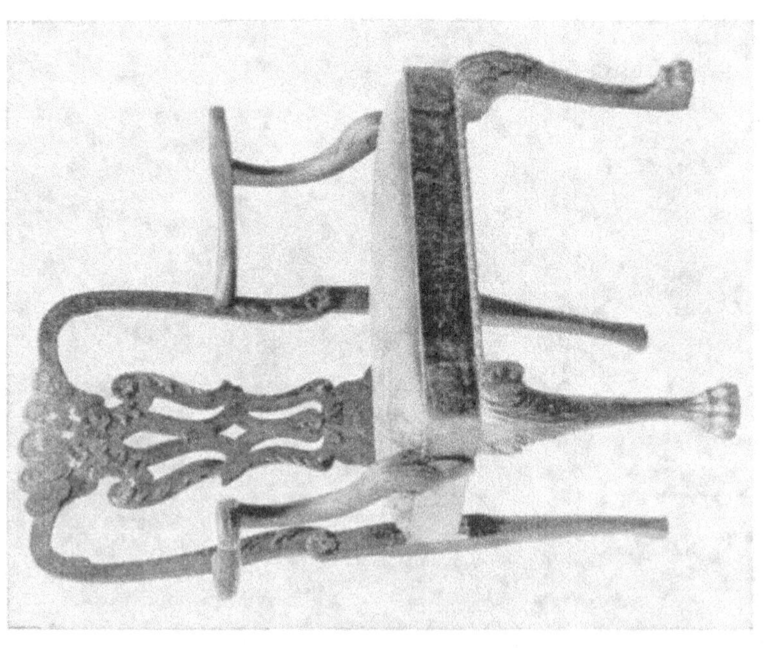

WALNUT ARM CHAIR, ENGLISH, *c. 1730.* PIERCED CENTRAL SPLAT; PAW FEET

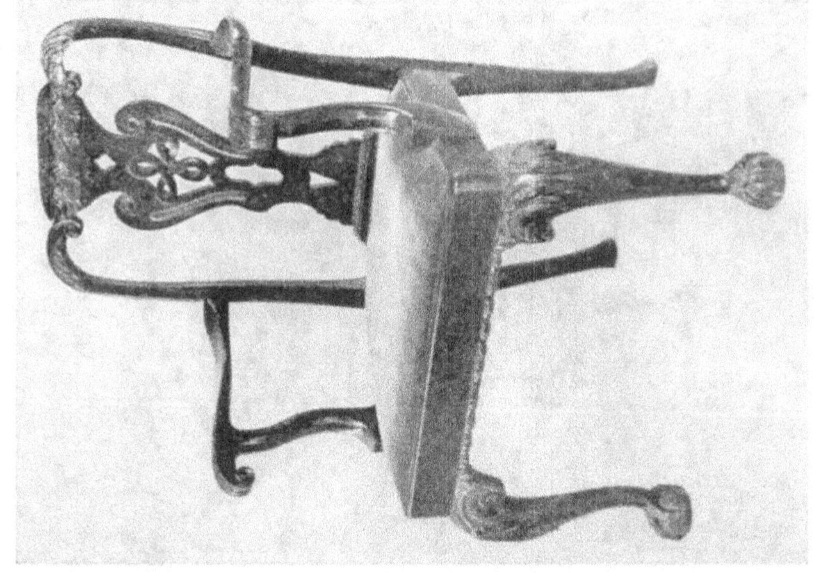

MAHOGANY ARM CHAIR, ENGLISH, *c. 1735.* THE HOOP-BACK PERSISTING IN THE MAHOGANY YEARS

CABRIOLE CHAIRS OF THE EARLY MAHOGANY PERIOD

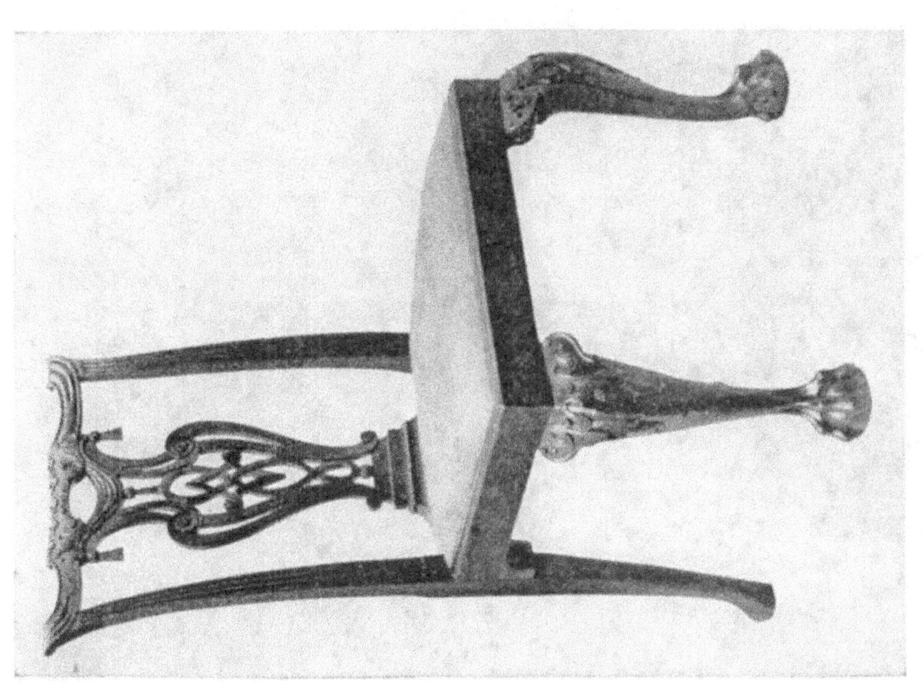

CHAIR, ENGLISH, *c. 1740.* INTERLACED CENTRAL SPLAT

CHAIR, ENGLISH, *c. 1745.* NOTE THE CARVING AND SHAPING OF THE FRONT SEAT RAIL, A DETAIL RARE IN ENGLISH BUT USUAL IN PHILADELPHIA CHAIRS

CABRIOLE CHAIRS OF THE EARLY MAHOGANY PERIOD

CHAIR, ENGLISH, *c. 1745.* A DEFINED TYPE; TOP RAIL BOLDLY SPIRALLED AT JUNCTIONS WITH ARMS; ELABORATELY INTERLACED CENTRAL SPLAT. A STYLE NEVER COPIED IN AMERICA

CABRIOLE CHAIR OF THE EARLY MAHOGANY PERIOD

ARM CHAIR, ENGLISH, *c. 1745.* LION MASKS ON ENDS OF ARMS AND KNEES OF LEGS; PAW FEET; SIMPLE PIERCED CENTRAL SPLAT

ARM CHAIR, ENGLISH TYPE OF *c. 1745.* KNEES OF CABRIOLE LEGS CRESTING OVER SEAT FRAME; SCROLL FEET. SIMPLE PIERCED CENTRAL SPLAT

CABRIOLE CHAIRS OF THE EARLY MAHOGANY PERIOD

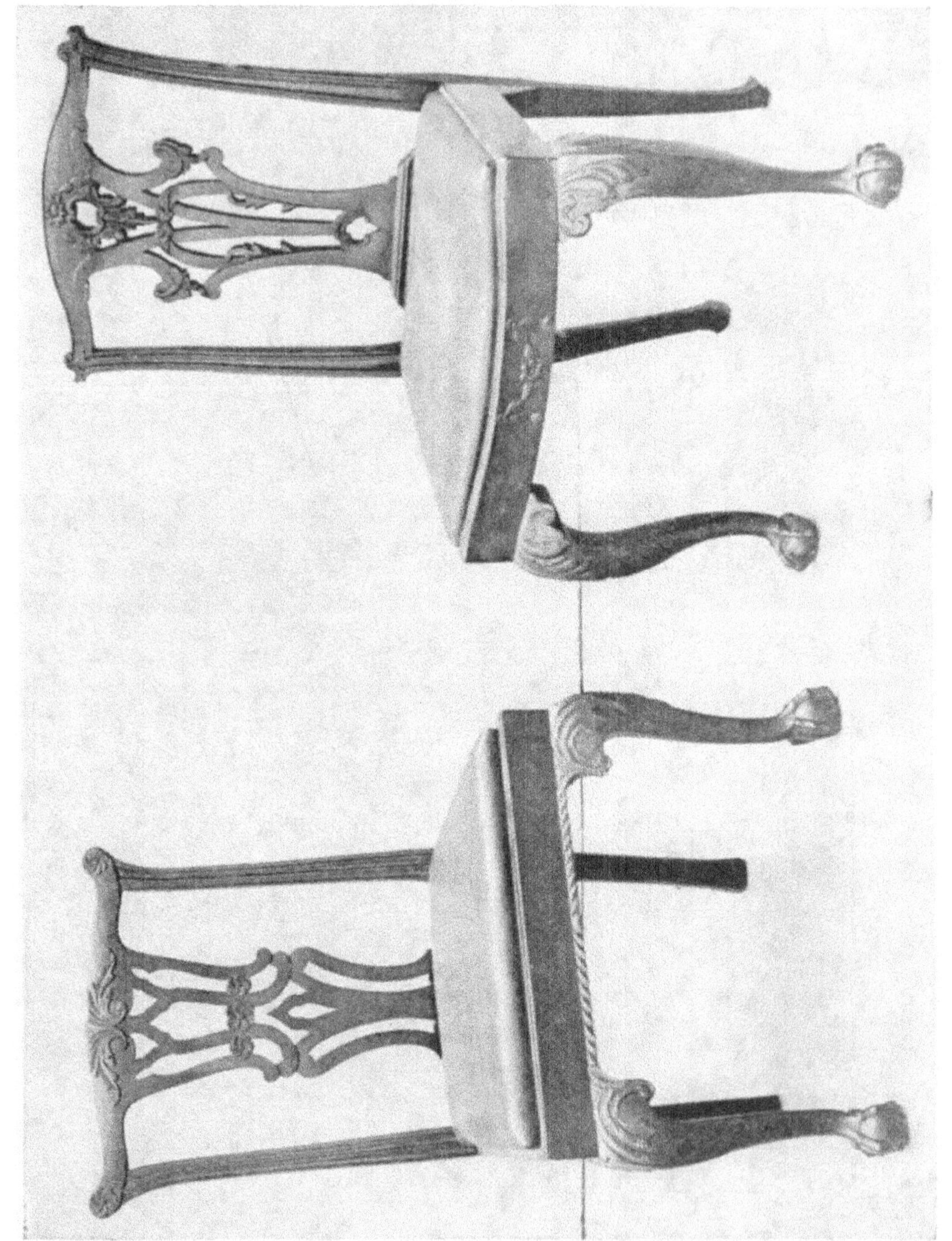

COMPARE THESE CHAIRS WITH THOSE OF PHILADELPHIA, AND NOTE THE VARIOUS DIFFERENCES, ESPECIALLY IN THE BACK LEGS

ENGLISH CABRIOLE CHAIRS OF THE CHIPPENDALE SCHOOL

ARM CHAIR, ENGLISH, *c. 1735–40.* LION MASKS ON ENDS OF ARMS AND KNEES OF FRONT LEGS. NOTE THE CARVING OF THE "APRON" TO FRONT OF SEAT RAIL

CABRIOLE CHAIR OF THE EARLY MAHOGANY PERIOD

BEECH CARVED AND GILT ARM CHAIR, ENGLISH, *c. 1745.* UPHOLSTERED IN SOHO TAPESTRY, SCROLL AND LEAF-CARVED FOOT

CABRIOLE CHAIR OF THE EARLY MAHOGANY PERIOD

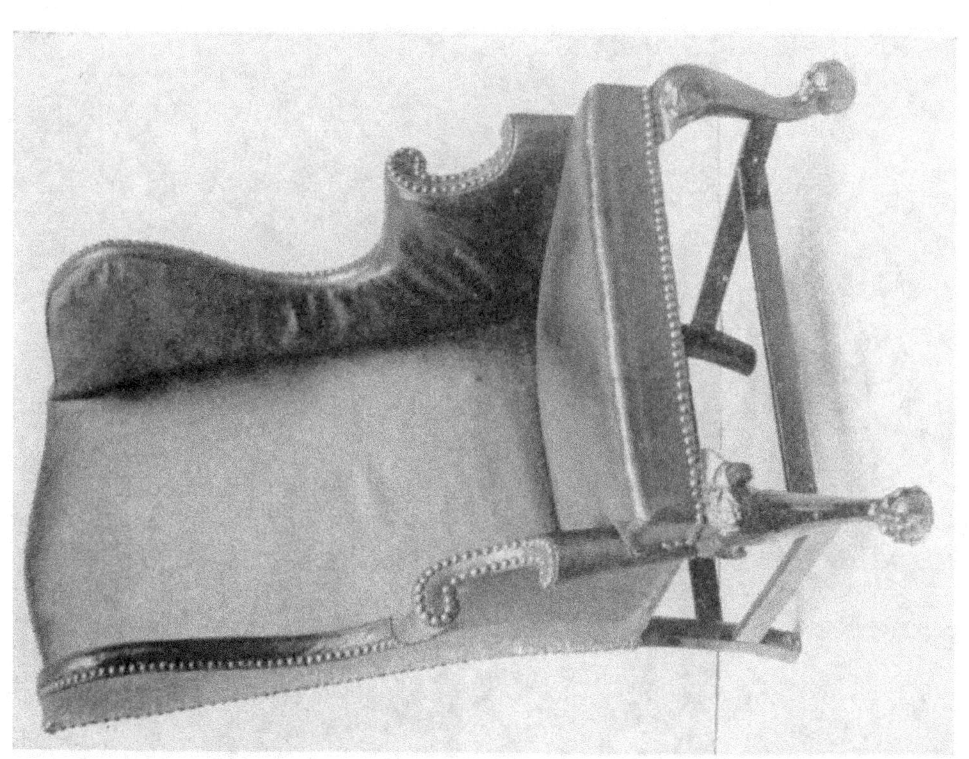

MAHOGANY WING CHAIR, ENGLISH, *c. 1740.* NOTE THE PERSISTENCE OF THE STRETCHER UNDER-RAILING BETWEEN THE LEGS

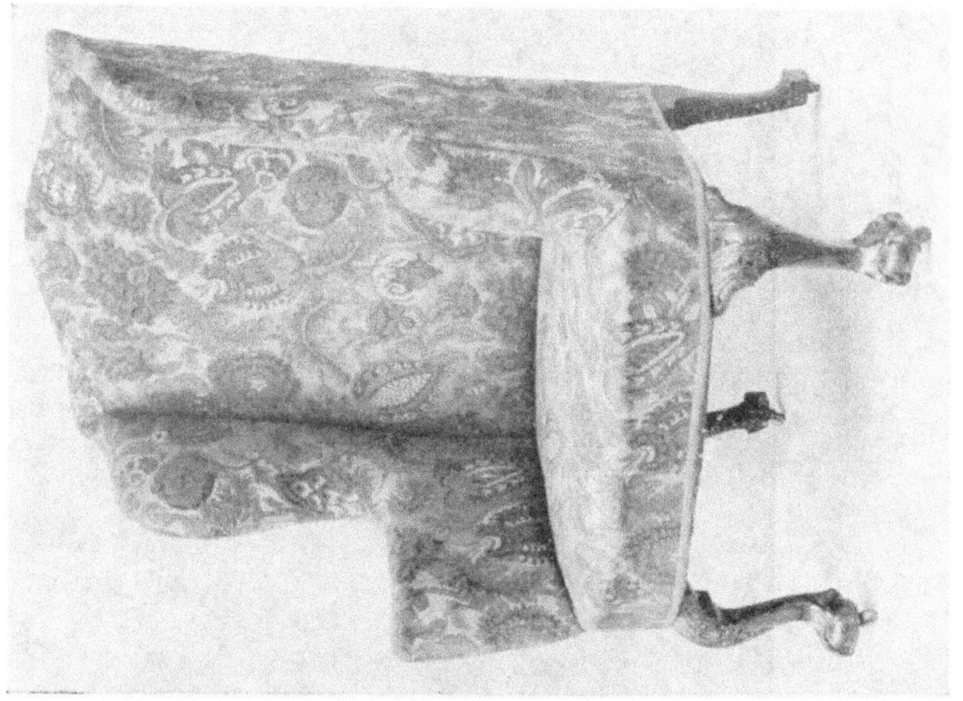

MAHOGANY WING CHAIR, ENGLISH, *c. 1750.* BALL-AND-CLAW FEET LEGS CARVED ON KNEES

CABRIOLE EASY CHAIRS OF PRE-CHIPPENDALE PERIOD

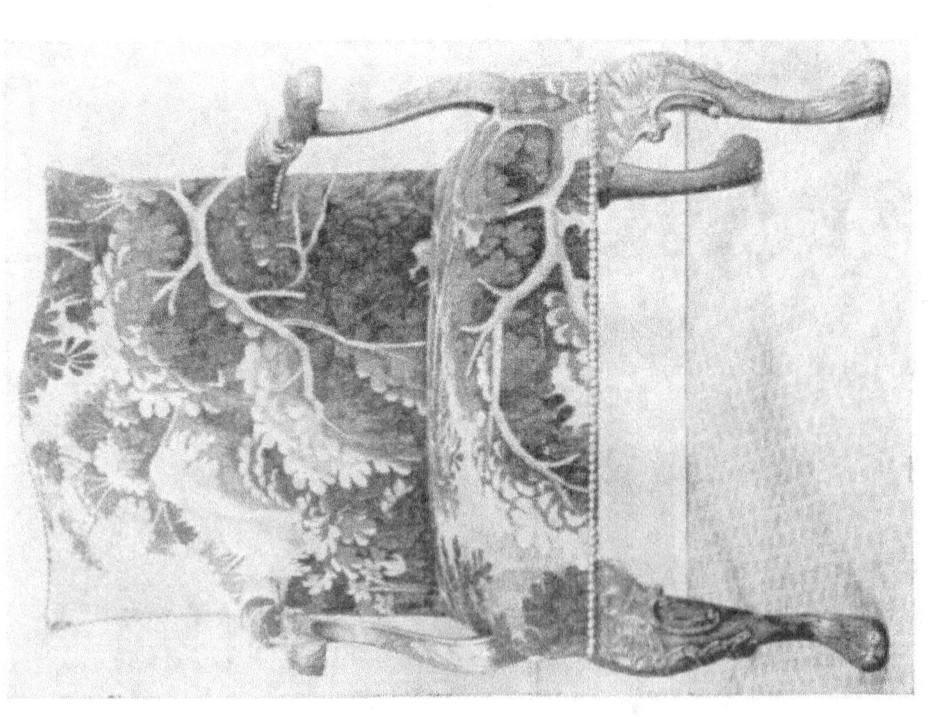

CARVED GILT ARM CHAIR, ENGLISH STYLE, OF *1750*. THE LEAF-CARVED FOOT

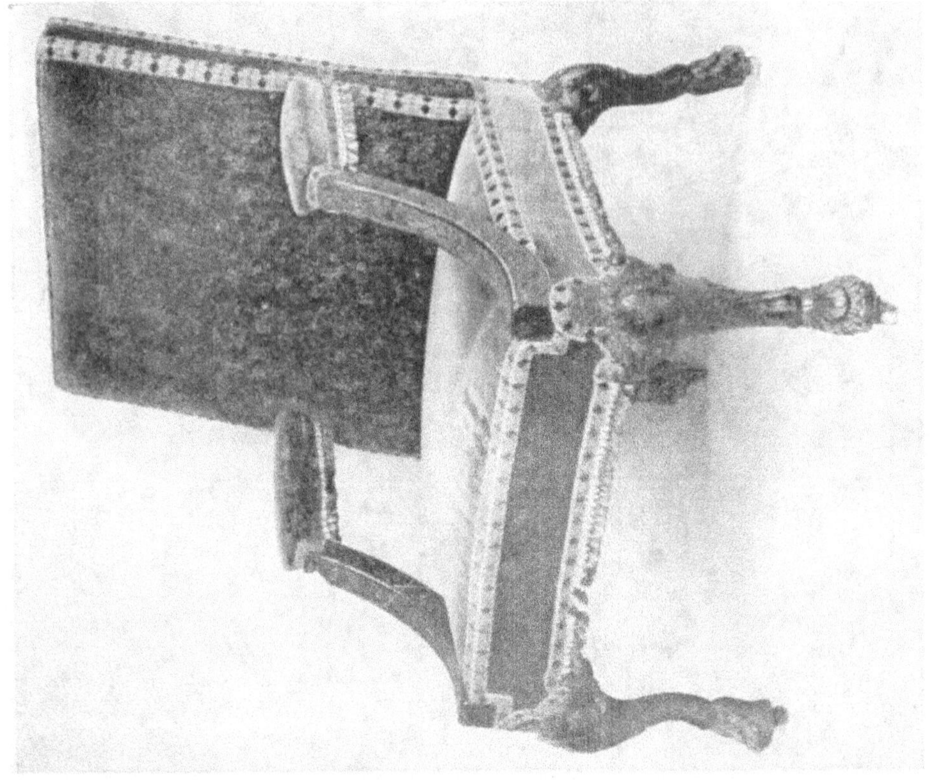

ARM CHAIR, ENGLISH, *c. 1745*. EXAMPLE OF THE CABOCHON-AND-LEAF ON THE KNEES OF THE FRONT LEGS

CABRIOLE CHAIRS OF THE EARLY MAHOGANY PERIOD

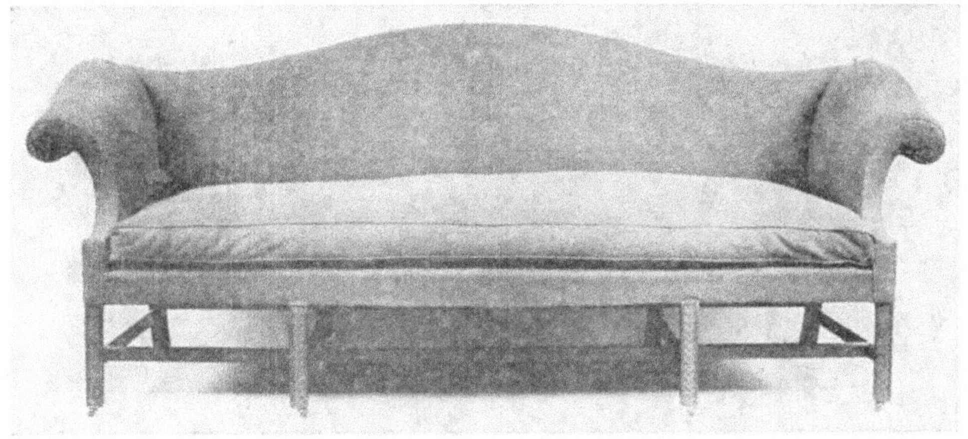

MAHOGANY SCROLL-ENDED COUCH OR SETTEE, ENGLISH, *c. 1750.* THIS TYPE WAS MADE FROM *1750* TO *1780*

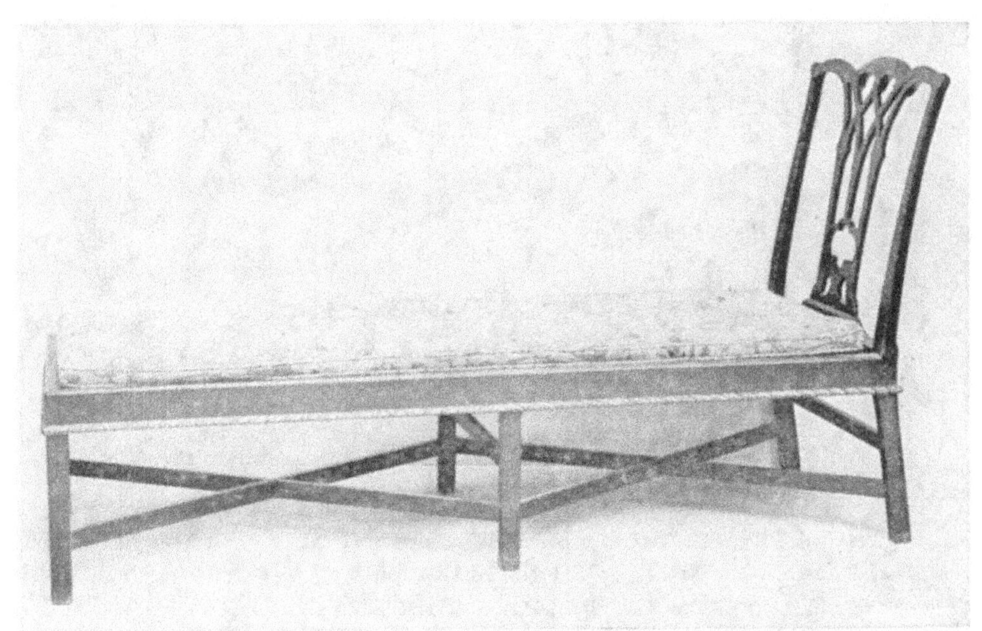

BIRCH DAY-BED, AMERICAN. STYLE OF CHIPPENDALE

SQUARE LEG CHIPPENDALE CHAIR AND SETTEE

MAHOGANY ARM CHAIR IN THE FRENCH MANNER OF THE CHIPPENDALE SCHOOL, BUT WITH EARLIER DETAILS INTRODUCED. COVERED WITH FULHAM TAPESTRY, *c. 1750–5*

ENGLISH CABRIOLE CHAIR OF THE CHIPPENDALE SCHOOL

Mahogany bergère chair, English. Chippendale style of *c. 1755*

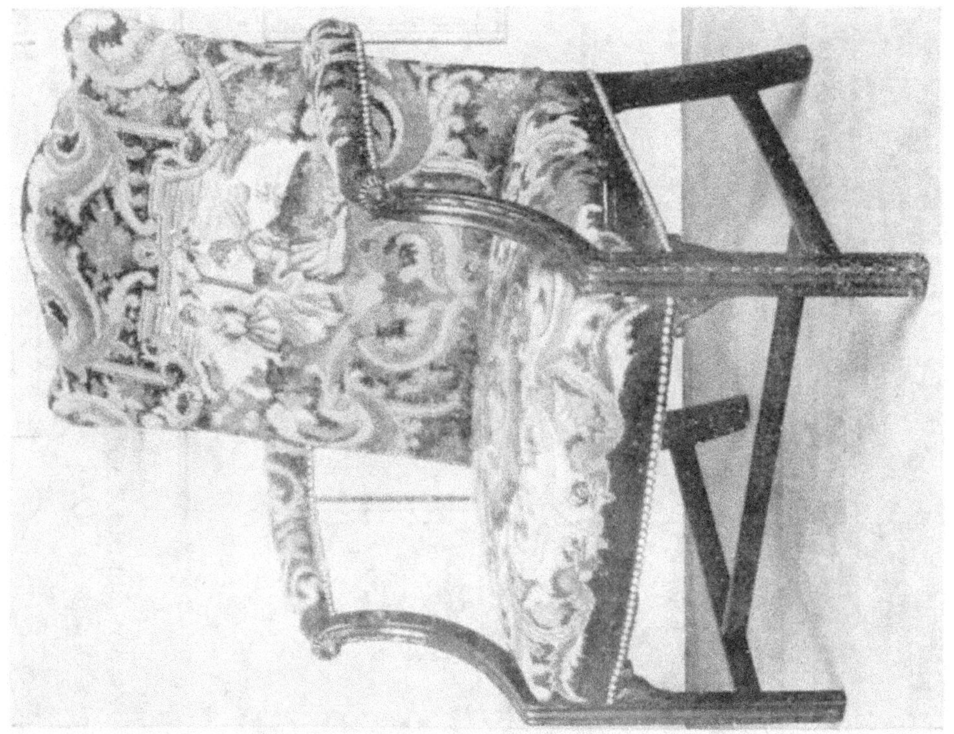

Mahogany bergère chair, English. Chippendale style of *c. 1755*

SQUARE-LEG BERGÈRE CHAIRS IN THE CHIPPENDALE STYLE

MAHOGANY BERGÈRE CHAIR, ENGLISH. STYLE OF CHIPPENDALE *c. 1755.* FRETTED UNDER-RAILING

MAHOGANY BERGÈRE CHAIR, ENGLISH. STYLE OF CHIPPENDALE *c. 1755.* TURNED UNDER-RAILING

MAHOGANY ARM CHAIR, ENGLISH, *c. 1755.* IN THE CHINESE MANNER OF CHIPPENDALE. THE LEGS OF TRIPLE CLUSTER COLUMNS

MAHOGANY ARM CHAIR, ENGLISH, *c. 1755.* THE CHIPPENDALE GOTHIC STYLE

MAHOGANY ARM CHAIR, ENGLISH, *c. 1755.* THE CHINESE CHIPPENDALE SCHOOL

MAHOGANY ARM CHAIR. ENGLISH STYLE OF *c. 1750.* THE OLDER INTERLACED BACK PERSISTING

SQUARE-LEG CHAIRS IN THE CHIPPENDALE STYLE

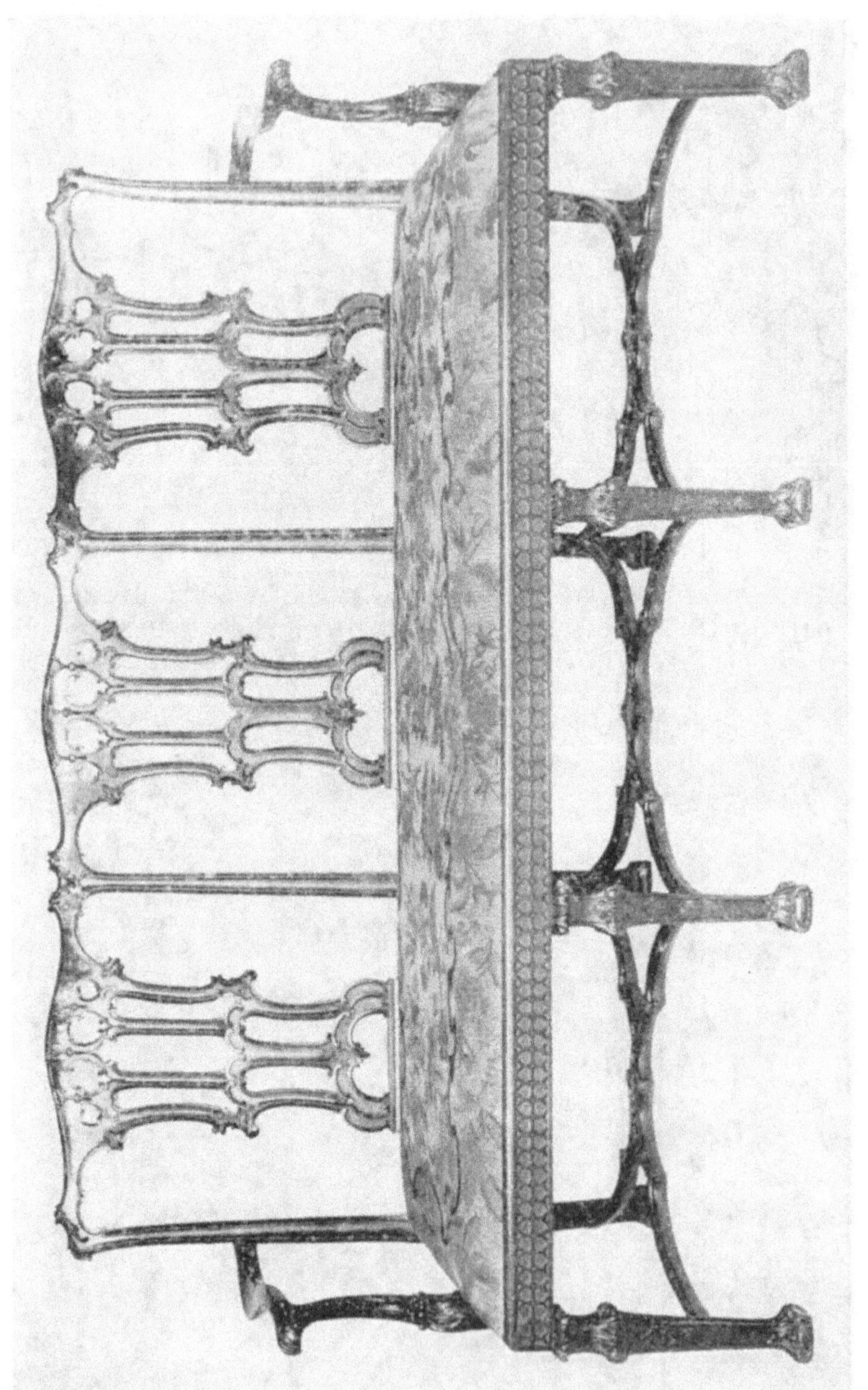

MAHOGANY SETTEE. CHIPPENDALE GOTHIC STYLE, ENGLISH, *c. 1755*. NOTE THE PERSISTENCE OF THE EARLY WILLIAM AND MARY FLAT STRETCHER

ENGLISH SETTEE IN THE CHIPPENDALE SQUARE-LEG STYLE

MAHOGANY SIDE CHAIR, ENGLISH, *c. 1760.* INTRODUCING THE "RIBBAND-BACK" WHICH WAS NEVER COPIED IN AMERICA. NOTE THE STYLE OF THE BACK LEG AND COMPARE WITH PHILADELPHIA

MAHOGANY CABRIOLE CHAIR OF THE CHIPPENDALE SCHOOL

MAHOGANY CHAIRS, ENGLISH, *c. 1755.* THE EARLIER INTERLACED CENTRAL SPLAT AS ADOPTED BY THE CHIPPENDALE SCHOOL

MAHOGANY CHAIR, ENGLISH, *c. 1760.* DEFINED TYPE OF CHIPPENDALE SCHOOL. NOTE EARLY TYPE OF STRETCHERING

MAHOGANY CHAIR, ENGLISH, *c. 1760.* THE INTERLACED SPLAT PERSISTING

SQUARE-LEG CHAIRS IN THE CHIPPENDALE STYLE

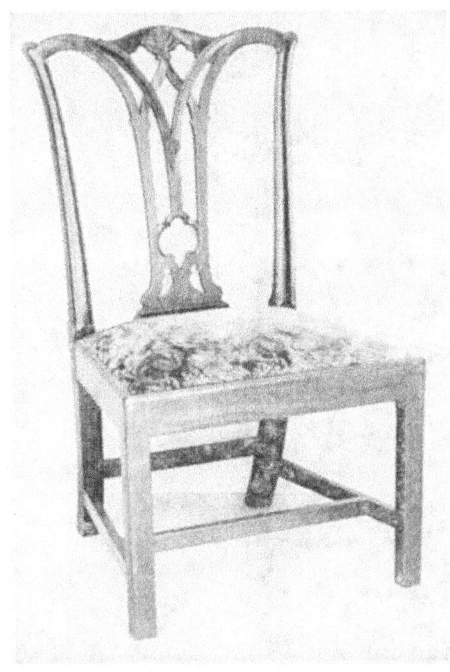

MAHOGANY CHAIR, ENGLISH, *c. 1760.* THIS STYLE WAS EXACTLY COPIED IN PHILADELPHIA IN *1780*

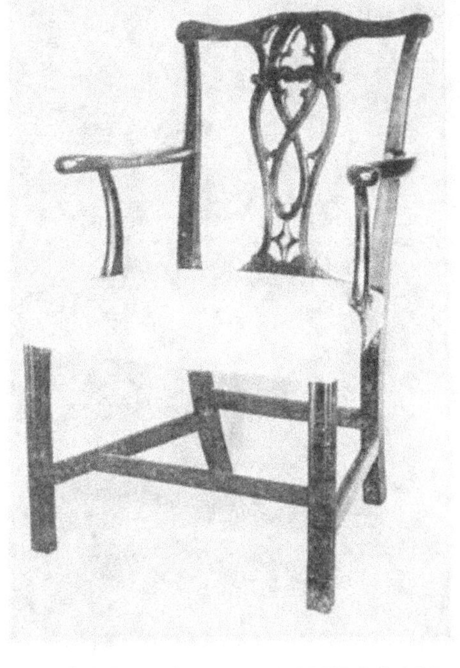

MAPLE CHAIR, AMERICAN, *c. 1770.* PROBABLY OF NEW ENGLAND MAKE

MAHOGANY ARM CHAIR, ENGLISH, *c. 1760.* ELABORATELY CARVED; INTERLACING CENTRAL SPLAT

MAHOGANY ARM CHAIR, ENGLISH, *c. 1755.* THE GOTHIC MANNER OF CHIPPENDALE. THE EARLIER STYLE OF ARM AND SUPPORT

SQUARE-LEG CHAIRS IN THE CHIPPENDALE STYLE

MAHOGANY SIDE CHAIR, *c. 1770.* THE BACK ALMOST A LITERAL COPY FROM THE ENGLISH, BUT WITH THE STUMP BACK LEG AND THE TYPICAL CUT-OUT SEAT

PHILADELPHIA CHIPPENDALE CHAIR

EXAMPLES OF THE TYPE GENERALLY ATTRIBUTED TO SAVERY, *c. 1775*

PHILADELPHIA CHIPPENDALE CHAIRS

MAHOGANY WING CHAIR, *c. 1770.* PROBABLY FROM PENNSYLVANIA

CABRIOLE CHAIR, AMERICAN TYPE

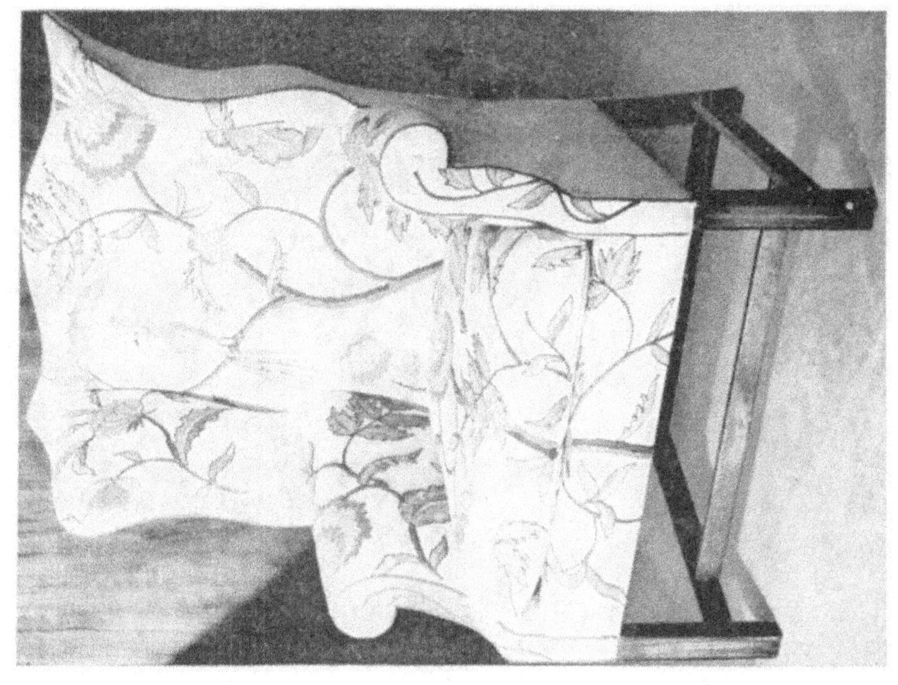

MAHOGANY WING CHAIR, *c. 1780.* IN THE STYLE OF THE CHIPPENDALE BERGÈRE

DRAPED WING ROCKING CHAIR. NEW ENGLAND TYPE OF THE LATE *18*TH CENTURY

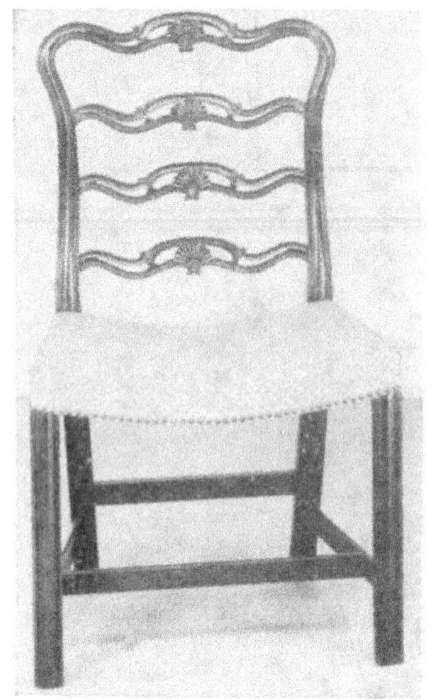

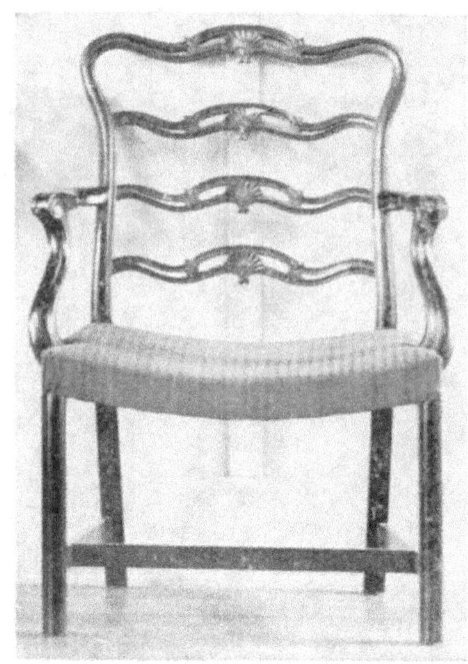

THE LADDER-BACK WITH SQUARE LEGS
AND THE OLD HOOP-BACK PERSISTING

MAHOGANY LADDER-BACK CHAIR, AMERICAN. THE NEW ENGLAND HIGH BACK

MAHOGANY LADDER-BACK CHAIR. SHOWING THE ENGLISH PROPORTION OF BACK

MAHOGANY CHIPPENDALE LADDER-BACK CHAIRS

MAPLE, WITH RUSH SEAT

MAPLE, DISPROPORTIONATELY HIGH BACK

THE REFINED TYPE

MAPLE. A STURDY SIMPLE TYPE

NEW ENGLAND TYPES OF CHIPPENDALE CHAIRS

CHAPTER VIII

AMERICAN AND ENGLISH DADO FURNITURE

COMMODES, CHESTS OF DRAWERS, LOW-BOYS, BUREAUX

THE RESTORATION BED ROOM

IN FRANCE an expressive term, *meuble d'appui,* is used to describe all wall furniture of leaning height, and for this we have no equivalent in English. This *meuble d'appui* includes chests of drawers, commodes, low-boys, side tables, bureaux and desks, so it is fairly comprehensive. For want of a corresponding term in general use, I have coined the one of "dado furniture" which is clumsy, and far from being clear in its meaning, without explanation, but which is employed in this chapter for want of a better.

In England, the commode practically coincides with the mahogany years, from about 1735 onwards. It begins as a bed room piece, for use as a dressing table with separate swing toilet mirror above. Since the Restoration, the bed room had become one of the important rooms in the house, in which the lady held formal morning receptions, perhaps because it was the only room in which one person, at least, (the occupant of the bed) could be assured of keeping warm. It was anything but a private chamber, as the huge elaborate bedsteads of the period indicate. It maintained this importance—and publicity—until almost the close of the eighteenth century, after which the "four-poster" went out of fashion. These draped bedsteads were devised for semi-privacy rather than as a defense against draughts, and they must have been horribly stuffy in summer weather. At the same time, they are decorative pieces of furniture, especially those of the Restoration period, in their glory of velvet, silk, fringe, braid and tassel, and they remained in favor with the settlers of New England, (but probably for other reasons) until nearly 1800. Three examples are illustrated here to give some idea of the amount of work which was lavished upon them. Those of the eighteenth century, shorn of valances and curtains, have an attenuated and unsatisfactory appearance, but one can imagine them in all their glory—like Solomon.

THE COMMODE

Many of these mahogany commodes are extremely elaborate, not only those made for the state rooms, but others which must have been intended as dressing tables or chests. Thus, in the latter, we find pedestals with a central cupboard (the latter sometimes made to pull forward on runners or slides and fitted inside with one or two shelves for shoes) which effectually denote the purpose for which the piece was made. This pedestal-and-cupboard, or "knee-hole" table as it is known, begins in the early walnut years, and one sometimes finds the Queen Anne pieces with lifting lids and fitted inside with a hinged and strutted mirror, powder and patch boxes, and other articles of the toilet. In the later mahogany years, after about 1750, this lifting lid was replaced by a top drawer made to pull out on runners (to support it when fully extended) with similar fittings inside. The separate swing dressing glass, on side pillars with cross stretcher, is a rare piece of furniture before the late Hepplewhite period, *circa* 1788–95. Another exceptional article before 1785 is the cheval glass, but Chippendale gives designs for screens on this principle, known at the time as "horse-screens."

To the same family as the commode belongs the pedestal writing table, especially of the kind made with drawers on the front only, to stand against a wall. As a rule, however, these tables have drawers or cupboards both at back and front, and in the Metropolitan Museum is a superb table (it is illustrated in this chapter) which is "four-way," probably made for the use of four partners in a business. It is to be hoped they did not quarrel; friction at such close quarters might be disagreeable, and persistent.

The commode being merely a glorified chest of drawers, persists in an unglorified form, although in Pennsylvania these chests of drawers are often fine examples of craftsmanship, detail and proportion. At the same period the lower drawer is removed and replaced by carved cabriole legs, and we get the low-boy. These pieces appear to have had a triple use; they served as dressing tables in the bed room, as side tables in the dining room, and, in New England, the top drawer is sometimes hinged on the front, to fall down, and pull out, for use as a secretary, the interior being fitted with small drawers, pigeonholes, etc. Philadelphia held the high position with these cabriole-leg low-boys, those from Connecticut or Massachusetts being usually crude copies, and with light woods, such as maple, substituted for mahogany. There are some pieces, and the high-boy and the low-boy are examples, which lose much of their fine character when translated into light woods, even when the same quality of detail, proportion and workmanship is retained.

Rhode Island and Newport, the home of a fine school of makers, of whom John Goddard is generally regarded as the apostle, do not appear to have taken kindly to the low-boy form, preferring either the chest or the pedestal table as being better adapted for the display of the block-front. The slant-front desk, or bureau, also reaches its finest limit in the work of this school.

ACCURACY IN TERMS

THE bureau begins as an English piece, in the first years of the seventeenth century, although, at this date, writing could not have been a common accomplishment. At first it is merely a small desk with a lifting lid, made to stand on a table.

To keep terms within comprehensible limits, I object to the name "desk," as used in America, to indicate pieces as varied as a writing table, a bureau, a secretary or a slope-fronted chest with an upper part in cabinet or bookcase form. This is the country of precise expression, *par excellence,* and it were time that the word "desk" were used to indicate one piece, a slope-fronted box made for writing, where the slope is hinged at the back, and made to lift up. Where the sloping fall is hinged at its base, made to be supported on pull-out "runners" or "lopers," I prefer the term "bureau." Where the fall is upright, when closed, made to let down on side quadrants, that is a *secrétaire* or secretary. A flat-top "desk" is a writing table; when supported on pedestals instead of legs, it is a pedestal writing table. Thus we get secretary or bureau cabinets or bookcases, the former where the doors are solid paneled, or, if glazed, where the interior is shelved for china or similar objects, the latter where the doors have glass, either in latticed panes or in one sheet, with shelves made movable in grooves, or on pins or slips, to accommodate various sizes of books. It is only by the use of such precise terms that confusion can be avoided.

AMERICA'S BEST

ALTHOUGH these Philadelphia high-boys and low-boys bring enormous prices at public auctions, if I were asked to select the finest examples of American furniture, in the last half of the eighteenth century, my choice would fall on the block-fronted bureaux from Newport and Rhode Island. To my mind they are at once the best and the most logical of all the American pieces, with the exception of similar, and plainer pieces, made on the banks of the Delaware at about the same period, in which the walnut of the locality was substituted for the imported mahogany.

DRAPED STATE BED, IN VELVET AND EMBROIDERIES. FROM RUSHBROOK HALL. OAK FRAMING, *c. 1685*

ENGLISH FOUR-POSTER BEDSTEAD

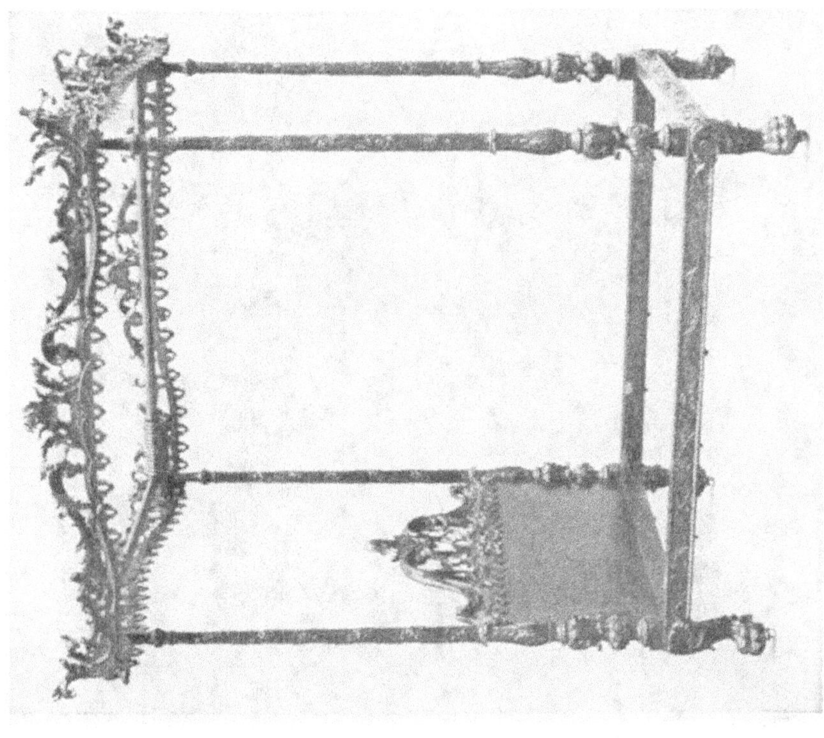

MAHOGANY BEDSTEAD, *c. 1750–60*. THE FULL STYLE OF THE CHIPPENDALE SCHOOL

MAHOGANY BEDSTEAD, *c. 1780*

BOTH BEDSTEADS ON THIS PAGE ARE EXCEPTIONAL IN HAVING FINISHED POSTS AT ALL FOUR CORNERS. AS A RULE THOSE AT THE HEAD WERE PLAIN SQUARES, INTENDED TO BE COVERED BY THE CURTAINS AND BACK-CLOTH OF THE BEDSTEAD HEAD

ENGLISH FOUR-POSTER BEDSTEADS

MAHOGANY SERPENTINE-FRONTED COMMODE OR DRESSING CHEST, WITH CENTRAL SHOE CUPBOARD, *c. 1755–60.* ORIGINAL HANDLES

ENGLISH MAHOGANY COMMODE OF THE CHIPPENDALE PERIOD

MAHOGANY SERPENTINE-FRONTED COMMODE IN THE ROCOCO MANNER OF CHIPPENDALE. ALTHOUGH ORNATE, THIS WAS MADE, ORIGINALLY, TO SERVE AS A DRESSING CHEST. ORIGINAL HANDLES. *c. 1755*

ENGLISH MAHOGANY COMMODE OF THE CHIPPENDALE PERIOD

MAHOGANY COMMODE, ENGLISH, 1755

FORMERLY AT RAINHAM HALL, NORFOLK, THE SEAT OF THE MARQUIS OF TOWNSHEND. THIS PIECE FIRST FIGURES IN THE RAINHAM INVENTORY IN *1756*

MAHOGANY "FOUR-WAY" PEDESTAL WRITING TABLE, *c. 1755*. GRECIAN KEY-BORDER IN FRIEZE, COVERING DRAWERS WITH REBATED FRONTS AND CONCEALED JOINTS OVERLAPPING THE DRAWER STILES. THE TOP IS FRAMED UP AND LINED WITH BLACK LEATHER. THE WORK OF THE CHIPPENDALE SCHOOL

ENGLISH PEDESTAL WRITING TABLE

MAHOGANY WARDROBE, *c. 1755.* REPRODUCED FROM ONE-HALF OF THE DOUBLE DESIGN ON PLATE *104* OF THE FIRST EDITION (*1754*) OF CHIPPENDALE'S "DIRECTOR"

MAHOGANY WARDROBE OF THE CHIPPENDALE PERIOD

MAHOGANY COMMODE, *c. 1760.* THE FRENCH MANNER OF THE CHIPPENDALE SCHOOL

MAHOGANY LOW-BOY. AMERICAN, *c. 1770.* PHILADELPHIA MAKE

ENGLISH COMMODE AND AMERICAN LOW-BOY

MAHOGANY OF *c. 1770.* THE ALMOST IDENTICAL CHARACTER OF THE TWO SUGGESTS A COMMON WORKSHOP ORIGIN

BLOCK-FRONTED CHESTS OF RHODE ISLAND

MAHOGANY LOW-BOY, *c. 1770*

MAHOGANY LOW-BOY, *c. 1770*

PHILADELPHIA MAHOGANY LOW-BOYS

CURLY MAPLE LOW-BOY, PENNSYLVANIA, SOUTH OF THE DELAWARE, *c. 1750*. THE FINE SIMPLE EARLY TYPE

MAHOGANY AND CHERRYWOOD LOW-BOY, *c. 1770*. THE LATER ORNATE TYPE

PENNSYLVANIA LOW-BOYS

WALNUT LOW-BOY

MAHOGANY LOW-BOY

PENNSYLVANIA LOW-BOYS

MAHOGANY LOW-BOY, *c. 1760.* SIMPLE BUT REFINED TYPE

MAHOGANY CHEST OF DRAWERS, *c. 1760.* TYPICAL QUAKER MODEL

PHILADELPHIA MAHOGANY FURNITURE

MAHOGANY BLOCK-FRONTED CHEST OF *1770*. SHOWN HERE TO LARGE SCALE TO INDICATE THE TYPE OF UNFIGURED MAHOGANY WHICH WAS USED FOR THIS RHODE ISLAND FURNITURE

MAHOGANY CHEST OF DRAWERS FROM RHODE ISLAND

BUREAUX ON STANDS

WALNUT, ENGLISH TYPE OF *c. 1680*

POPLAR AND DEAL. NEW ENGLAND, *c. 1770*

AMERICAN WALNUT SLANT FRONT BUREAUX, PROBABLY MARYLAND OR VIRGINIA, *c. 1700–10.* COPIED FROM THE ENGLISH LATE *17*TH CENTURY TYPES

AMERICAN BUREAUX

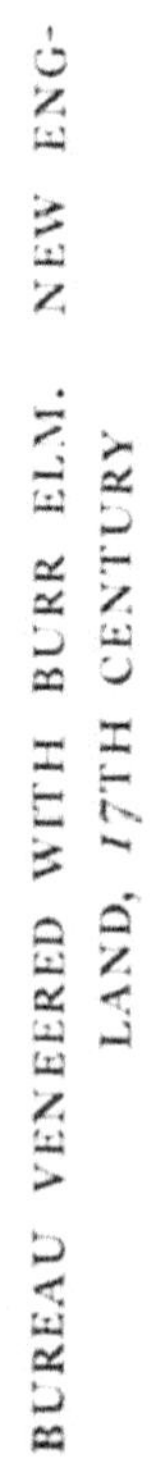

BUREAU VENEERED WITH BURR ELM. NEW ENGLAND, *17th* CENTURY

OAK AND WALNUT WRITING CABINET. NEW ENGLAND, *c. 1690–1700.* A DIRECT COPY OF AN ENGLISH FASHION

AMERICAN BUREAU AND WRITING CABINET

MAHOGANY BUREAU ON CABRIOLE STAND. PROBABLY RHODE ISLAND OF *c. 1740*

AMERICAN BUREAU ON STAND

CHERRYWOOD BUREAU, CRUDE TYPE OF *c. 1740*

NEW ENGLAND SLANT-FRONT BUREAU

PINE AND CHERRY

MAHOGANY

COPIES OF ENGLISH TYPES, EARLY *18*TH CENTURY

NEW ENGLAND BUREAUX

MAHOGANY BLOCK-FRONTED. LIFTING HANDLES AT SIDE, RHODE ISLAND, *c. 1760–70*

MAHOGANY SERPENTINE FRONTED, PHILADELPHIA, *c. 1770*

AMERICAN BUREAUX

MAHOGANY, DOUBLE SERPENTINE FRONT. PHILADELPHIA, *c. 1770*

MAHOGANY BLOCK-FRONTED. RHODE ISLAND, *c. 1760*

AMERICAN BUREAUX

MAHOGANY, RHODE ISLAND, *c. 1780.* SAID TO HAVE BEEN MADE FOR BRIG. GEN. EBENEZER HUNTINGTON OF NORWICH, CONN. (*1754–1834*)

THE MAHOGANY BUREAU, DATED *1769*, ON FOLLOWING PAGE, HERE SHOWN OPEN

AMERICAN BUREAUX

MAHOGANY BUREAU, DATED *1769*. FINE EXAMPLE OF RHODE ISLAND DESIGNING

MAHOGANY BUREAU FROM RHODE ISLAND

PHILADELPHIA TYPE OF *c. 1770*

RHODE ISLAND, *c. 1750.* UNUSUAL IN HAVING BRACKET FEET

AMERICAN MAHOGANY BUREAUX

MAHOGANY AND SATINWOOD. HEPPELWHITE STYLE, *c. 1790.* PROBABLY NEW YORK

LATER AMERICAN CHESTS OF DRAWERS

CHAPTER IX

DOUBLE CHESTS, HIGH-BOYS AND CABINETS

CLASSIFYING FURNITURE

FOR the sake of convenience of classification, furniture may be divided into four main categories: (1) that made to stand against the wall, (2) that made to hang on it, (3) that made to stand on the floor and away from the wall, and (4) chairs, sofas, settees, stools and the like. We may call the first "wall furniture" and the second "mural furniture." The third comprises tables of all kinds, writing tables, desks, bureaux and similar pieces, and the fourth is obvious.

The wall furniture can be subdivided into high pieces, and those of dado or chair-rail height. The former comprises double-chests, wardrobes, bookcases, china cabinets, corner cupboards, bureau and *secrétaire* cabinets and what are known in England as "tallboys" and in America as "high-boys." Furniture and woodwork merge, almost insensibly the one into the other, and if we include the latter, the field can be widely extended.

Dado furniture consists of certain slant-front or fall-front writing desks or chests (in England these are known as bureaux and *secrétaires* respectively), side tables, sideboards, serving tables, dressing and washing tables, chests of drawers, and that typically American piece, the low-boy, which is midway between the chest and the table. To include dressing or washing tables in this category is straining a point, perhaps, as the definition of a wall piece should be one where the back is left, more or less, in an unfinished state; not polished like the front.

THE CHEST-ON-STAND

IN SPITE of the obvious inconvenience of mounting one chest of drawers on another (which necessitates the use of a step-ladder to inspect the contents of the top drawer) this piece, whether as double chest with base or plinth, or elevated on a stand or on legs (the high-boy in America, the chest-on-stand of England) seems to have enjoyed a wide popularity in the two countries from the last quarter of the seventeenth almost until the close of the eighteenth century. It is to be found, in England, in oak, walnut and mahogany, (rarely, if ever, in satinwood) and in America, especially in the New England states, in the same woods, with maple, cherry, butternut, elm and other woods, used almost haphazard, and often assorted in the one piece.

In England, in the first years of the eighteenth century, when the cabriole had just come into fashion, it is not unusual to find these double chests on cabriole legs, but the fashion was only a short-lived one, and belongs only to the country districts, especially of the Midlands. Such pieces are never found in mahogany, yet they served as the prototypes for the later New England and Pennsylvania high-boys, although it must be pointed out that it is only the idea which is adopted; there is little or no kinship between a Philadelphia high-boy and anything ever made in England.

The English seventeenth century model of chest on a stand with drawers, shaped apron, turned legs and flat stretcher was often copied with the utmost fidelity in the New England states, and such evidences as wood and constructive methods are often the only indications of American workmanship in origin. There is no doubt that some of these pieces were actually imported from England in the later years of the seventeenth century, as household chattels which served, at a later date, as models for the woodworking settlers. From these up to the high-boy with cabriole legs (nearly always made from mahogany) of Rhode Island and Philadelphia, there is almost an unbroken evolutionary chain. The earliest of the New England pieces are those with the drawer fronts enriched with elaborately mitered mouldings, in the late English Jacobean manner, the next development being where forms of the inverted cup-turning are used. The latter is a typical Orange detail, beginning in England, about 1690, and, in that country, nearly always associated with walnut; very rarely with oak.

WOODS FOR INTERIORS

One striking difference between the English and the New England chests, whether low or high, is that the interiors of the drawers in the former are invariably of oak, and quarter-sawn lumber of fine figure, whereas the latter are nearly always of pine or deal, rarely of poplar or maple. In this respect the American pieces copy from the original Dutch prototypes, where white pine was the usual wood for interior and carcase work.

During the latter half of the eighteenth century, especially in Rhode Island and Philadelphia, this early practice was often abandoned, and one finds drawer sides of oak, mahogany and even walnut, no rule or fashion appearing to govern the selection of carcase woods.

It is hardly necessary to point out that the use of deal or pine, in this chest furniture, is a proof neither of nationality nor date, as the "Early American" piece made the day before yesterday does not err in this particular.

AMERICAN HIGH-BOYS

THE high-boys of Philadelphia and Rhode Island stand in a class apart, shared only with the low-boys which were often made as pendant pieces, and of identical design. There is some evidence to show that, in certain instances, the high-boys began as low-boys, the upper stages being added later, probably to order. In both localities these pieces were of the finest quality, workmanship and material. The wood nearly always was a fine close-grained Cuban mahogany, of great weight and free from figure. In rare cases, cherry was substituted for mahogany, either wholly or in part.

High-boys and low-boys were also made in Connecticut and in Massachusetts, but these examples are greatly inferior to those of Philadelphia or of Newport, and curly maple was generally used instead of mahogany. The hardware, the drawer and cupboard brasses, is also inferior and of lighter weight.

One is prone to attach too great a significance to names, forgetting that even the presence of a maker's label is not absolute proof of origin. Labels can become detached, and be affixed in other places and to other pieces. In one instance, it is known that this actually happened. There is no doubt, however, that Philadelphia makers did label their furniture, in many cases and two chairs, one with the label of William Savery, the other with that of Benjamin Randolph, exist, and are beyond question. Several of these labeled pieces have been found and authenticated. In spite of this, however, we know very little of the characteristics of each maker's work, nor are we sure that any such exists. Who made these fine Philadelphia high-boys; William Savery, Benjamin Randolph, Jonathan Gostelowe, or some other makers whose history, advertisements, labels or business cards have not been preserved? Of one thing we can be reasonably certain; the reckless attribution of these elaborate high-boys to William Savery—a practice which has hitherto been general—is entirely without warrant. Savery may have been one of the finest of the Philadelphia makers (we are not certain even of this), but we know that he had only a small establishment even at his death in 1787, not to be compared with that of Randolph.

It is safe to assume that many of these pieces have the stamp of one man's work, or, more correctly, that they emanated from the one workshop, but that is as far as one can go with safety.

THE BLOCK-FRONT

ANOTHER elusive maker is John Goddard of Newport who has, similarly, been credited with every piece of block-fronted furniture which has ever been found. He may have originated the device of the block-front (in its developed form it is never found in English furniture at any period), but these pieces may well have been the work of a school rather than of a single man or an individual workshop. That the type was extremely localized, in Rhode Island, it is possible to believe, as there were many historical reasons which would have precluded the dissemination of a new style at this date. The fashion does not even appear to have penetrated into Connecticut or Massachusetts, which one would have expected.

Cut from the solid wood, without veneering, and with the consequent end grain where the block-front begins to project or recede, the style would hardly be a popular one with the lighter woods such as maple, as this end grain would shade badly when the piece was polished or varnished. It is practicable only in the timber which was actually used, hard and heavy Cuban mahogany.

WALNUT CHEST ON SPIRAL-LEG STAND INLAID WITH "SEAWEED" MARQUETERIE, *c.* 1675

WALNUT WRITING CABINET WITH FALL-FRONT, DECORATED WITH PANELS IN THE "CHINESE TASTE." EARLY *18*TH CENTURY

ENGLISH CHESTS AND CABINETS

OAK, ENGLISH WITH FLEMISH INFLUENCE,
c. 1690

VENEERED WITH BURR WALNUT, POSSIBLY
PENNSYLVANIA. EARLY *18*TH CENTURY

CHESTS OF DRAWERS ON STANDS, ENGLISH AND AMERICAN

WALNUT, MASSACHUSETTS, *c. 1700*. ENGLISH TYPE OF *c. 1690*

WALNUT, MASSACHUSETTS. EARLY *18*TH CENTURY. ENGLISH LATE *17*TH CENTURY TYPE

VENEERED WITH YEW TREE BURRS, CONNECTICUT VALLEY, LATE *17*TH CENTURY

PINE, CONNECTICUT VALLEY, LATE *17*TH CENTURY

AMERICAN CHESTS OF DRAWERS ON STANDS

(LEFT) WALNUT, NEW ENGLAND. EARLY 18TH CENTURY. COPY OF ENGLISH LATE 17TH CENTURY

(RIGHT) CHERRY-WOOD, RHODE ISLAND. EARLY 18TH CENTURY

AMERICAN CHESTS OF DRAWERS ON STANDS

BEECH AND PINE, EARLY *18*TH CENTURY

NEW ENGLAND CHEST ON STAND

CARCASE OF MAPLE AND PINE. THE FRONTS OF THE DRAWERS VENEERED WITH FIGURED ASH. EARLY 18TH CENTURY. ENGLISH LATE 17TH CENTURY TYPE

ENGLISH CHEST ON STAND

CHERRYWOOD, EARLY *18*TH CENTURY

NEW ENGLAND CHEST ON STAND

(LEFT) WALNUT, PHILADELPHIA, MID-18TH CENTURY. THE ENGLISH QUEEN ANNE TYPE, BUT WITH THE AMERICAN DETAIL OF THE CUT-OUT SKIRT

(RIGHT) VENEERED WITH VIRGINIA WALNUT. PROBABLY PENNSYLVANIA. EARLY 18TH CENTURY

AMERICAN CHESTS ON CABRIOLE STANDS

FIGURED MAPLE HIGH-BOY ON CABRIOLE STAND. SOUTHERN NEW ENGLAND, *c. 1740.* THE FIRST APPEARANCE OF THE SHAPED PEDIMENT

HIGH-BOY WITH SHAPED PEDIMENT

(RIGHT) MAHOGANY BUREAU CABINET WITH BOMBÉ LOWER STAGE. FINEST POSSIBLE QUALITY. PROBABLY NEWPORT, *c. 1760*

(LEFT) MAHOGANY BUREAU CABINET. PHILADELPHIA WORK OF FINE QUALITY. THIRD QUARTER OF THE *18*TH CENTURY

THE WORK OF AMERICAN CABINETWORKERS

MAHOGANY BUREAU CABINET WITH FRETTED PEDIMENT, *c. 1765*

THE WORK OF PHILADELPHIA CABINETMAKERS

MAHOGANY DOUBLE CHEST WITH FRETTED PEDIMENT, *c. 1770*

THE WORK OF PHILADELPHIA CABINETMAKERS

(RIGHT) MAHOGANY, *c. 1770.* PROBABLY BY BENJAMIN RANDOLPH. COMPARE THE SIMILAR CONSTRUCTION OF THE TWO PEDIMENTS ON THIS PAGE

(LEFT) MAHOGANY, *c. 1770.* PROBABLY BY JONATHAN GOSTELOWE

PHILADELPHIA HIGH-BOYS ON CABRIOLE STANDS

(LEFT) MAHOGANY, *c. 1770.* COMPARE THE PEDIMENT AND THE QUARTER-ANGLE COLUMNS WITH THOSE OPPOSITE AND NOTE DIFFERENCES FROM THOSE ON PREVIOUS PAGE

(RIGHT) MAHOGANY OR CHERRY-WOOD, *c. 1770.* POSSIBLY THE WORK OF WILLIAM SAVERY. THE ORIGINAL BRASSES ARE MISSING

PHILADELPHIA HIGH-BOYS ON CABRIOLE STANDS

(RIGHT) MAHOGANY DOUBLE CHEST WITH PEDIMENT. BLOCK-FRONTED ON BOTH STAGES, WITH PROJECTING AND RECEDING FRONTS. THIRD QUARTER OF *18*TH CENTURY

(LEFT) MAHOGANY DOUBLE CHEST WITH PEDIMENT. LOWER STAGE BLOCK-FRONTED, MID-*18*TH CENTURY

THE BLOCK-FRONT OF NEWPORT AND RHODE ISLAND

(RIGHT) CHERRY WRITING CABINET WITH PEDIMENT. UPPER CARCASE PROBABLY OF LATER DATE. FEET NOT ORIGINAL. THIRD QUARTER OF THE *18*TH CENTURY

(LEFT) MAHOGANY WRITING CABINET WITH PEDIMENT. PROJECTING AND RECEDING ON ALTERNATE FACES ON THREE STAGES. THIRD QUARTER OF THE *18*TH CENTURY

THE BLOCK-FRONT OF NEWPORT AND RHODE ISLAND

MAHOGANY WRITING CABINET WITH PEDIMENT, RHODE ISLAND, OF *c. 1770.* OPENED TO SHOW THE ELABORATE INTERIORS OF THESE BLOCK-FRONTED PIECES

THE BLOCK-FRONT OF NEWPORT AND RHODE ISLAND

CHAPTER X

SIDE TABLES, SIDEBOARDS AND COMMODES

DEVELOPMENT OF SIDEBOARD

THE term "sideboard" is a misplacement rather than a misnomer. A "sideboard" literally, is a side table, but we have grown so accustomed to regard a sideboard as a piece of furniture with drawers or cupboards, made to contain cutlery, silver, napery or wine, that it is advisable to use the term in this sense here. The precursor, therefore, of the sideboard (used in this way) is the low oak "Suffolk" dresser of the late seventeenth century. Then follows a gap of nearly a century, in which the type does not recur. It requires considerable perceptive powers to notice the absence of certain pieces in the evolution of English furniture, yet this is immediately apparent when pointed out.

The sideboard with drawers and cupboards belongs to the period of Hepplewhite and his school, and is unknown before about 1780, in either the mahogany or the walnut years. The Queen Anne version is, first, the walnut side table, generally with a top of marble, then we get the early Georgian, where tables become more elaborate, are generally painted and parcel gilt, or entirely gilded, and to these years belong the console type, where the framing of the top is supported on front legs only, being secured, at the back, to the surbase or dado moulding. Included in this division is the top of marble, on a rectangular frame, supported on a carved eagle with outspread wings.

"IRISH CHIPPENDALE"

THE next development is the so-called "Irish Chippendale" which carries us into the mahogany years. It is curious how this name originated, and with whom; it has certainly been used *ad nauseam* by nearly all writers on this subject. I protested against it more than twenty years ago. It reminds me always of the *Saturday Evening Post,* which appears on Thursday, is not an evening paper nor a Post. Similarly, these pieces are not Irish (although they are to be found in Ireland, for reasons which will be explained shortly) and they are certainly prior to Chippendale.

Nearly everyone has heard of the Irish "absentee landlords," members of the British aristocracy who possessed large estates and houses in Ireland, which they seldom, if ever, visited, residing in England or Europe, and drawing back rents from that unhappy and poverty stricken country. To these great houses was dispatched, as a rule, any furniture which had become old fashioned or was not wanted. Towards the close of the eighteenth and the first half of the nineteenth centuries, many of the fine creations of the Chippendale and Hepplewhite schools were similarly regarded, and sent to these Irish mansions, yet no one has had the hardihood to declare this furniture as "Irish" because it was to be found in Ireland. It was only these mahogany tables with their peculiar surface-carved "aprons" or "skirts," which were thus regarded, and for no better reason. Actually, this was a short-lived, but well-defined western county fashion in England, and, curiously, was the prototype of many of the Philadelphia chairs and tables of *circa* 1770–80. This is immediately apparent to anyone comparing Philadelphia chairs with these "Irish" tables, yet no one would suggest inspiration from Irish sources for the former.

The type is so familiar, and so pronounced, that it is unnecessary to illustrate more than a single example here, but others of American origin, on the same and following page, will serve to emphasize the similarity in idea.

Perhaps no piece has been better understood or expressed than the Hepplewhite sideboard, in modern work, and six examples, from contemporary workshops, will illustrate this.

It is doubtful whether the credit for inventing the central side table with flanking pedestals, either detached or joined together, belongs to Adam or to Hepplewhite. Among the original Adam drawings in the Soane Museum, in Lincoln's Inn Fields, London, are several designs for these pedestal sideboards, but that is no proof that Robert or James Adam originated the type. It may well have been borrowed from the school of Hepplewhite, to which we know Robert Adam was greatly indebted for many of his furniture ideas.

THE COMMODE

If the important piece of the dining room be the sideboard, that of the drawing or state room, correspondingly, is the commode. We have seen how this developed in England, up to the period of Chippendale, transferring from the bed room to the sitting room, and how it became adopted in America as the low-boy. During the Adam, Hepplewhite and Sheraton periods, right up to the English Empire, in fact, it maintained its importance, and considerable designing skill and fine craftsmanship were lavished upon it. It developed all the more rapidly as the fashion changed from the earlier mahogany towards the use of the lighter woods, in veneers or inlay, or the painting of the flowers or medallions either on the wood or on prepared grounds of paint. A very delicate fashion was where the entire scheme was confined to varying tones of grey, *en grisaille,* as it was termed. In this late Adam period it became the custom to decorate the furniture not only in harmony with, but actually matching its background and this craze for "matching" had, often, rather dubious results. Thus at Osterly Park, Isleworth, near London, Robert Adam designed for Francis Child, the wealthy banker, ceilings which actually matched the carpets. It was, already, one of the design-weaknesses of the Brothers Adam that they made their ceilings far too ornate (it is the last part of a room which should be decorated, and it is more than doubtful if ceiling decoration, of any kind, be not an artistic error) and this matching of ceiling with the floor covering emphasized the offense; dotted the I's and crossed the T's of it, so to speak.

The commode was usually a piece of furniture made for ornament rather than use. Provided with either drawers or doors, (sometimes with both) it could have been made useful, but there are many signs which show that it was put to no definite purpose. It belongs to the *meuble d'appui*—furniture of dado height, which has been considered in Chapter VIII, and is carried on here in its sequence, to indicate its relationship to the side table and the sideboard. Like both Solomon and the lilies of the field, its function was to look beautiful, and in nearly every instance, it succeeded.

MAHOGANY SIDE TABLE, ENGLISH, *c. 1740.* THE SO-CALLED IRISH CHIPPENDALE

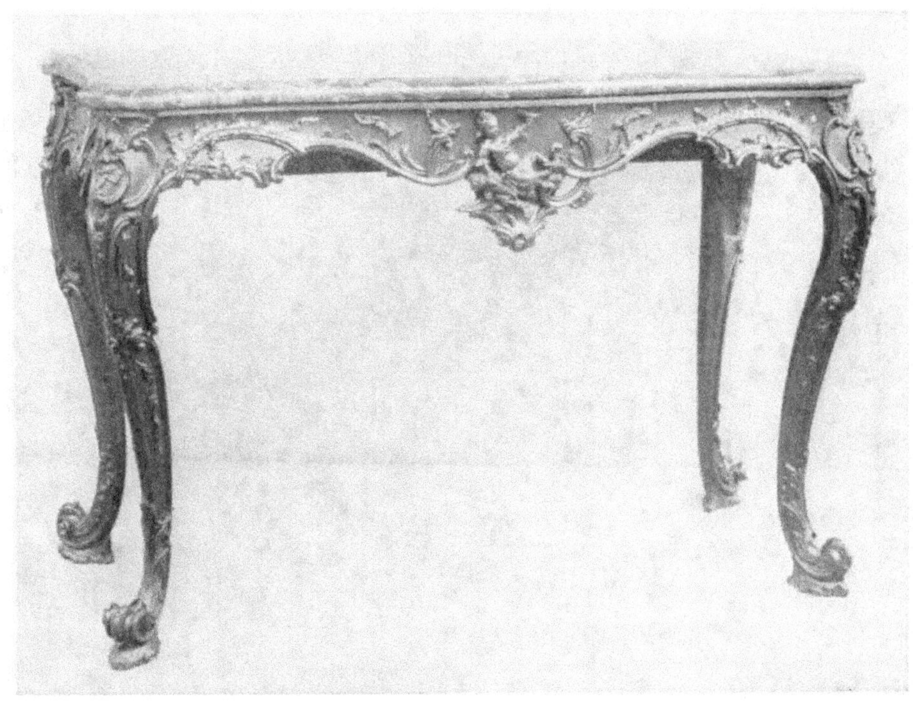

HARDWOOD TABLE, ORIGINALLY GILDED, WITH MARBLE TOP. PHILADELPHIA, PROBABLY BENJAMIN RANDOLPH, *c. 1775.* NOTE THE SIMILARITY IN INSPIRATION BETWEEN THIS AND THE TABLE ABOVE

ENGLISH AND AMERICAN SIDE TABLES AND SIDEBOARDS

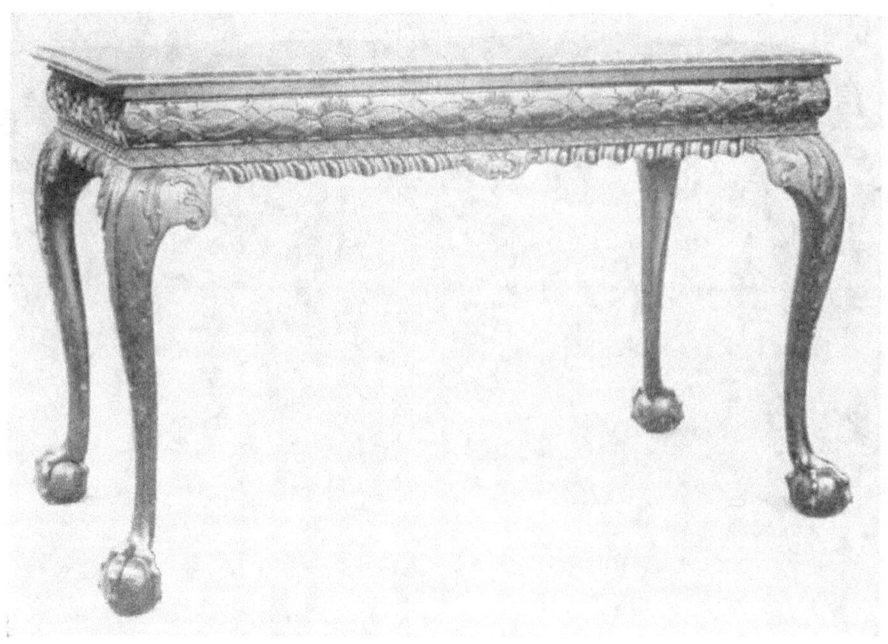

MAHOGANY SIDE TABLE WITH MARBLE TOP, PHILADELPHIA, *c. 1770–80.* CHIPPENDALE INFLUENCE

MAHOGANY VENEERED SIDEBOARD. AMERICAN, PROBABLY MARYLAND OR VIRGINIA, *c. 1800.* SHERATON OR HEPPLEWHITE INFLUENCE

AMERICAN SIDE TABLES AND SIDEBOARDS

INLAID WITH FANS AND STRINGING. MODERN RENDERING OF THE HEPPLEWHITE STYLE

MODERN MAHOGANY SIDEBOARD

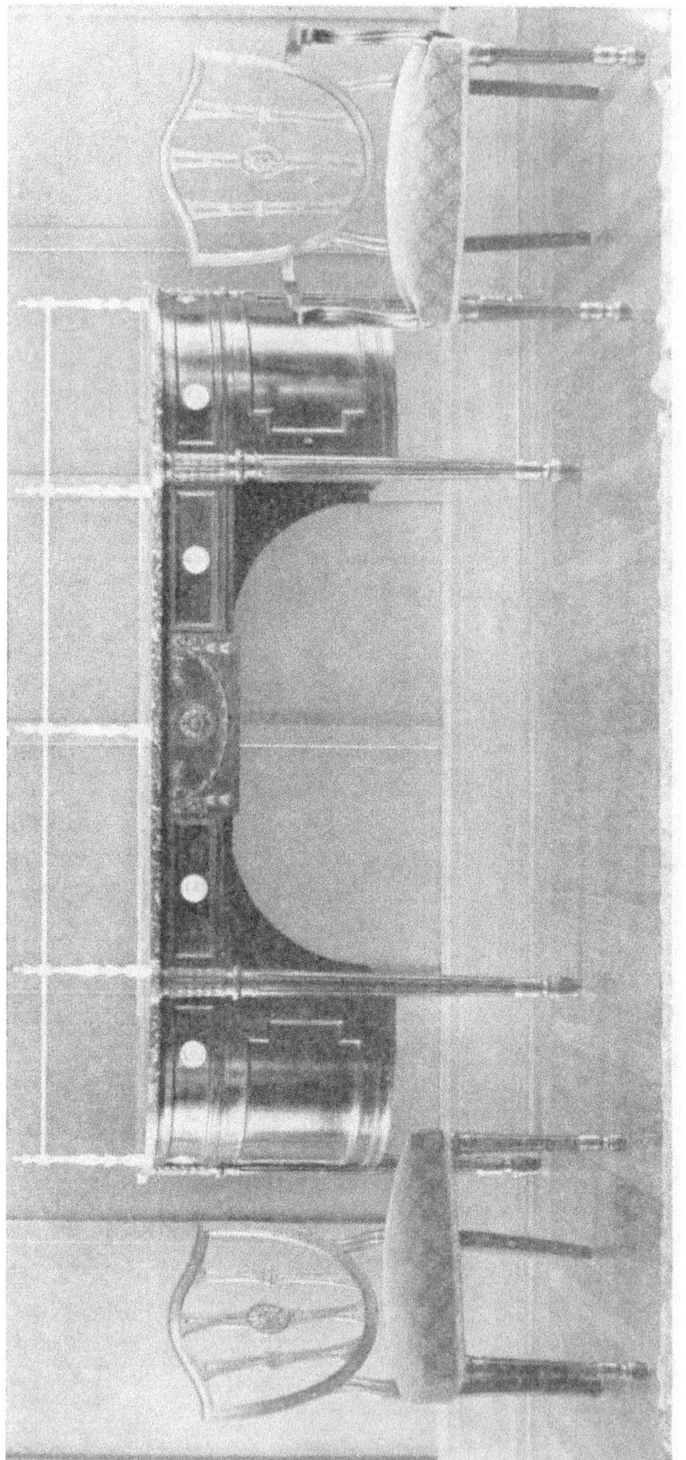

SIDEBOARD WITH MARBLE TOP AND BRASS BACK RAIL. MODERN FREE RENDERING OF THE ADAM-HEPPLEWHITE MANNER. THE CHAIRS ARE TYPICAL HEPPLEWHITE SHIELD BACKS

MODERN MAHOGANY SIDEBOARD AND CHAIRS

MODERN MAHOGANY SIDEBOARD

MODERN RENDERING OF THE HEPPLEWHITE STYLE UNDER AMERICAN INFLUENCE, INLAID

A MODERN RENDERING OF THE HEPPLEWHITE STYLE WITH REEDED LEGS

MODERN MAHOGANY SIDEBOARD

SIDE TABLE WITH FLANKING PEDESTALS. A MODERN FREE RENDERING OF THE ADAM STYLE

MODERN MAHOGANY PEDESTAL SIDEBOARD

ADAM-HEPPLEWHITE STYLE, *c. 1780*, WITH BRASS ENRICHMENTS

ENGLISH MAHOGANY SIDE TABLE

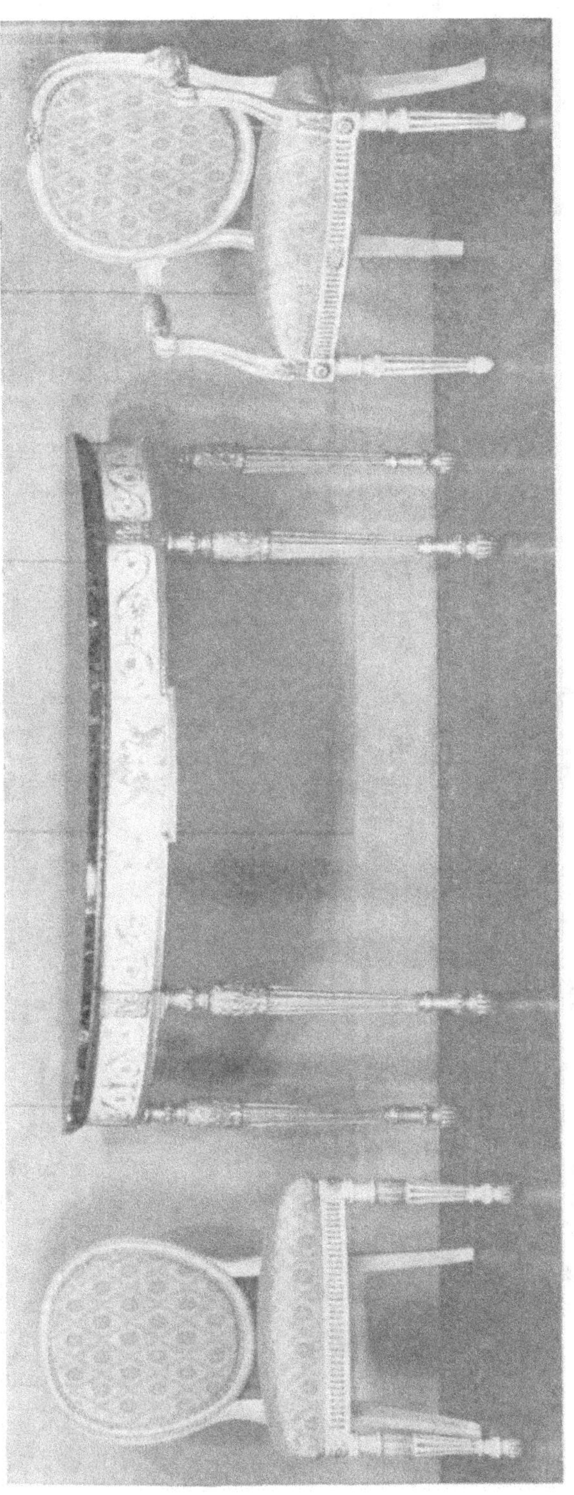

PAINTED AND PARCEL GILT ADAM-HEPPLEWHITE GROUP

ADAM-HEPPLEWHITE FURNITURE

PAINTED AND DECORATED COMMODE. MODERN COPY OF THE ENGLISH STYLE OF HEPPLEWHITE AND PERGOLESI OF *c. 1780–90*

MODERN COPY OF ENGLISH INLAID AND PAINTED COMMODE

COMMODE OF VARIOUS WOODS, INLAID WITH MARQUETERIE AND MOUNTED WITH ORMOLU, *c. 1770.* ADAM STYLE

COMMODE OF VARIOUS WOODS, INLAID WITH MARQUETERIE AND MOUNTED WITH GILT BRASS, *c. 1780.* THE FRENCH MANNER OF THE HEPPLEWHITE SCHOOL. SOME OF CHIPPENDALE'S WORK WAS IN THE SAME BOMBÉ STYLE

ENGLISH INLAID AND PAINTED COMMODES

SEMI-CIRCULAR COMMODE IN HAREWOOD AND SATINWOOD, WITH ENGRAVED INLAY OF FLOWERS, RIBBONS, FOLIAGE, HUSKS, VASES, *c. 1775.* STYLE OF ADAM-HEPPLEWHITE

ENGLISH INLAID AND PAINTED COMMODE

SEMI-CIRCULAR COMMODE OF SYCAMORE, CHESTNUT, KING-WOOD AND OTHER WOODS, INLAID WITH MARQUETERIE, *c. 1780–90.* STYLE OF HEPPLEWHITE

ENGLISH INLAID AND PAINTED COMMODE

CHAPTER XI

MAHOGANY TRIPOD FURNITURE

DATING THE TRIPOD

IN DEALING with the subject of furniture there is a strong temptation (and one which few writers withstand) to make positive statements which are only approximately true. Thus, it is near to the truth to say that the tripod is an innovation of the Chippendale school in England, and belongs to English furniture only from about 1750 onwards. Unfortunately for this theory, the stand or pillar table resting on three feet, is to be found in the marqueterie period, from 1670 to 1695, and in Holland (from whence it was borrowed) it is known for a decade or two prior to this. Many have seen the small stands, with octagonal tops and shafts, generally on bases to correspond, supported on three ball feet, or on three double scrolled legs. Sometimes these pieces are veneered with plain walnut; some are inlaid with marqueterie. Their nationality—whether English or Dutch—is often questionable, but, at this period, between the imported piece, the one made in England by Low Country workmen (who came to England in numbers in the years between 1690 and 1700) and the one made by English craftsmen copying from Dutch models, there is no very great distinction; certainly none which would be apparent in a photograph or an illustration.

Strictly speaking, therefore, the principle of the tripod was known in Holland in the middle of the seventeenth century, and in England some twenty years later. It only comes into definite fashion, in the latter country, nearly one hundred years later.

USE OF TRIPOD

A DEFINITE idea is embodied in the tripod form. A table or other article supported on four legs, will rock on an uneven floor; one with three only (a tripod) will rest firmly anywhere. For stands to support lamps or vases, therefore, three legs are preferable to four.

In the Chippendale period, the tripod was used for tables, for vase or candle stands (which are only elongated tables) for banner or pole screens, and, at a later date, for the pillar supports to large dining tables, or for others of smaller size with oval, round or rectangular tops. At the present day, the latter are usually termed "breakfast tables," on the principle that guests do not, as a rule, stay over night, and a smaller table only is required in the morning than on the night before.

It may be useful here to cite Earl Balfour's definition of a bore as "one who, invited to tea, stays to dinner." Presumably the tea-invited who remains to breakfast is a super-bore; certainly he may be a nuisance, which is much the same thing.

HOW DESIGNED AND MADE

It would be convenient if one could postulate any difference between the tripod furniture of England and America (bearing in mind that such differences would have to be manifest in an illustration, to be of any value), but this can only be done in extreme examples, choosing the best from the one country and the worst from the other. Good and bad tripods exist in both, but when they are bad, in England, it is a different kind of crudity to that of America. In a book of this nature, one has only space to illustrate representative specimens, and below a certain grade of artistic quality one cannot go. To do so would be merely using photographs to pad out a volume.

The tripod table consists of three elements: the top (which is nearly always detachable, made to revolve on the spindle of the pillar, in a "cage" of four columns) the central pillar, and the tripod stand, the two latter being fixed together. Occasionally, the top is fixed also, in which the "cage" is dispensed with. Where the "cage" is present, it consists of two square pieces (with a hole in the center of each to admit the spindle of the pillar) joined by four squat columns. In the pillar-spindle a slot is cut, into which a wedge of wood, projecting at both sides, is inserted, to secure the "cage" to the pillar. The top is hinged to this "cage" on pivots, and at the opposite end is a spring catch, or snap, which locks the top, when down, to its "cage," until released by the catch.

For this reason these tripods were known as "snap tables," in the eighteenth century.

Tops are either plain and flat, rectangular, square or round, or are enriched in several ways. The most usual is a dishing, with the edges of the top cut into two or three repeating shapes, and edged with a bead and a flat hollow, in the solid. This is commonly known as the "pie-crust," a name which expresses nothing in particular, and is copied, perhaps, from the small silver trays—"waiters," as they are styled—of the period. The next in order is the fretted gallery, (which has to be bent round a shaped top) the fret being generally laminated in three or five layers, in the manner previously described. Then we get the carved, splayed border, sometimes pierced, and lastly, the spindle gallery. Examples of each are illustrated here.

The stems or pillars during the Chippendale period, are curiously alike, compared with the diversity of the tops—a shaft, nearly always fluted, above a leaf-carved vase, and a classical type of base, finishing on the tripod itself. Rarely only is a variation attempted, where the pillar is in the form of a triple or cluster column. In the simple pieces, the pillar is merely turned, without carving, but these are becoming rare, as with later added embellishment, their commercial value is greatly increased. Thus the supply of ornate tripods increases, while the simple ones sensibly diminish in number.

The tripod of the Chippendale school is nearly always ogival, or cabriole as it is often incorrectly styled, but in the Hepplewhite, this form is reversed, the tripod resting on a tapered toe, on the floor, a form impossible with the Chippendale type. At a later date still the tripod is of a hollow, instead of an ogival form, and this takes us into the late Sheraton Empire style in England, and that of Duncan Phyfe in America, which will be considered later on. To this period belong the two- and three-tier dumb-waiters, which are rare with the ogival tripod, although one example is shown in the illustrations to this chapter.

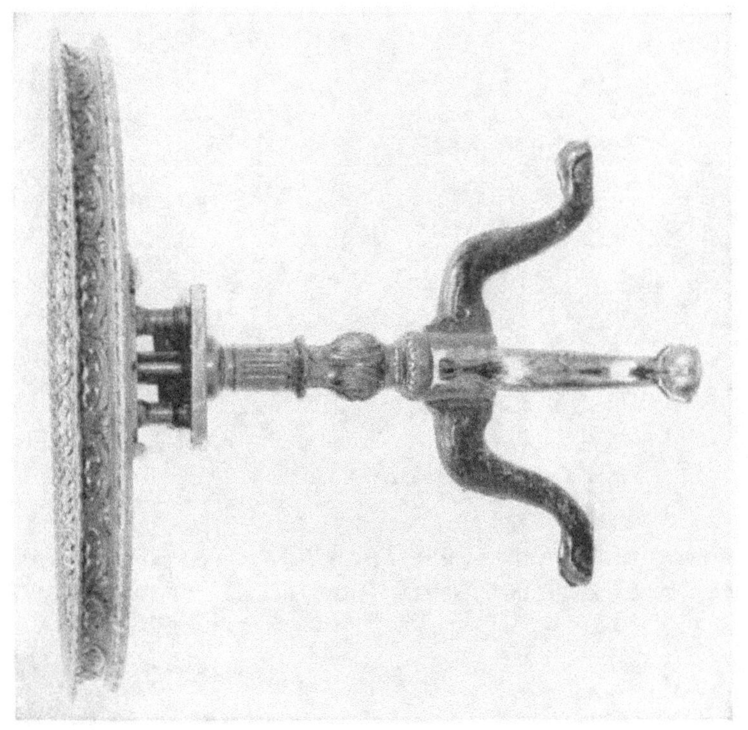

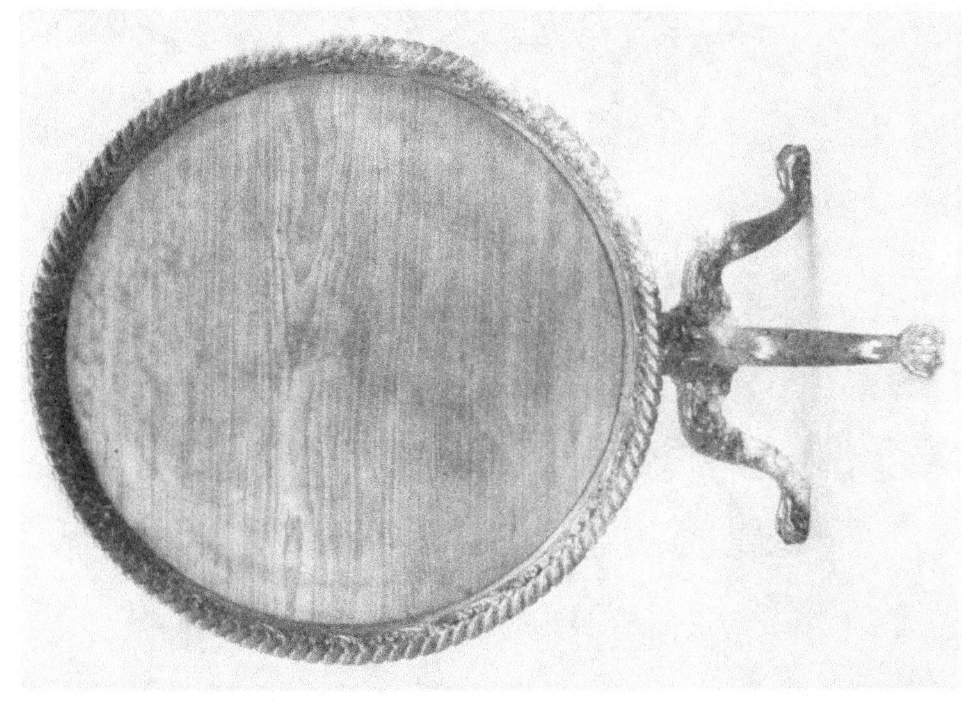

MAHOGANY TRIPOD TABLE, ENGLISH, *c. 1760.* SPLAYED, PIERCED AND CARVED GALLERY TO TOP. AT RIGHT, THE SAME TABLE WITH TOP TIPPED UP

TRIPOD TABLE OF THE CHIPPENDALE PERIOD

MAHOGANY TRIPOD TABLE. ENGLISH, *c. 1760.* THE "PIE-CRUST" TOP COPYING THE SILVER TRAYS OF THE PERIOD

TRIPOD TABLE OF THE CHIPPENDALE PERIOD

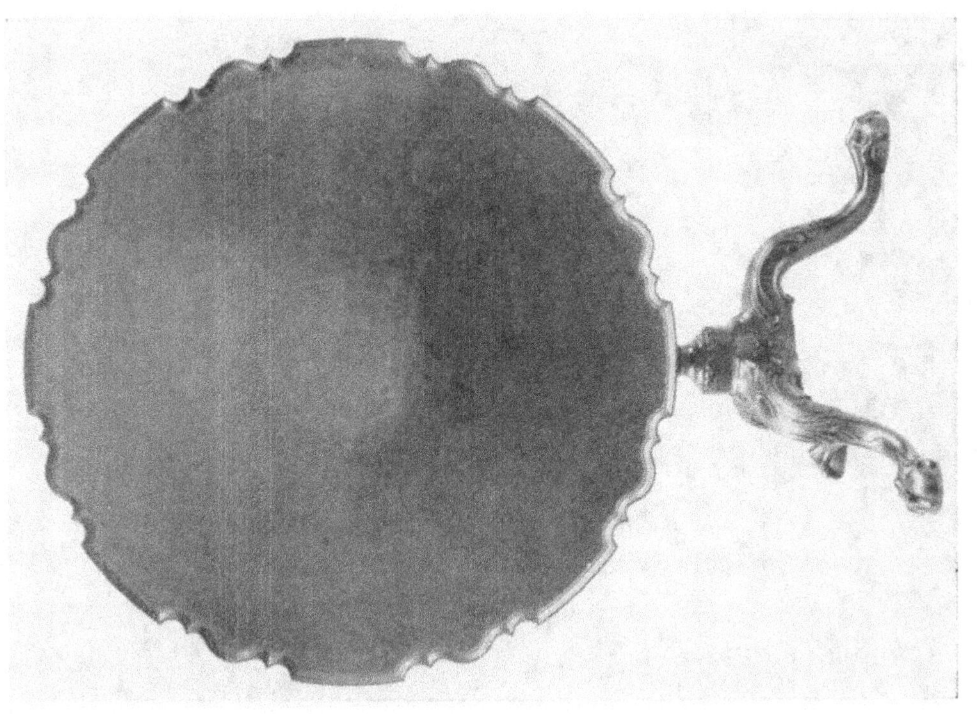

PIE-CRUST TOP, PHILADELPHIA

PIE-CRUST TOP WITH FLORAL ENRICHMENTS,
PROBABLY PHILADELPHIA

MAHOGANY TRIPOD TABLES, *c.* 1780

"PIE-CRUST" TOP, PHILADELPHIA, *c. 1770*

"PIE-CRUST" TOP, ENGLISH, *c. 1750*

MAHOGANY TRIPOD TABLES

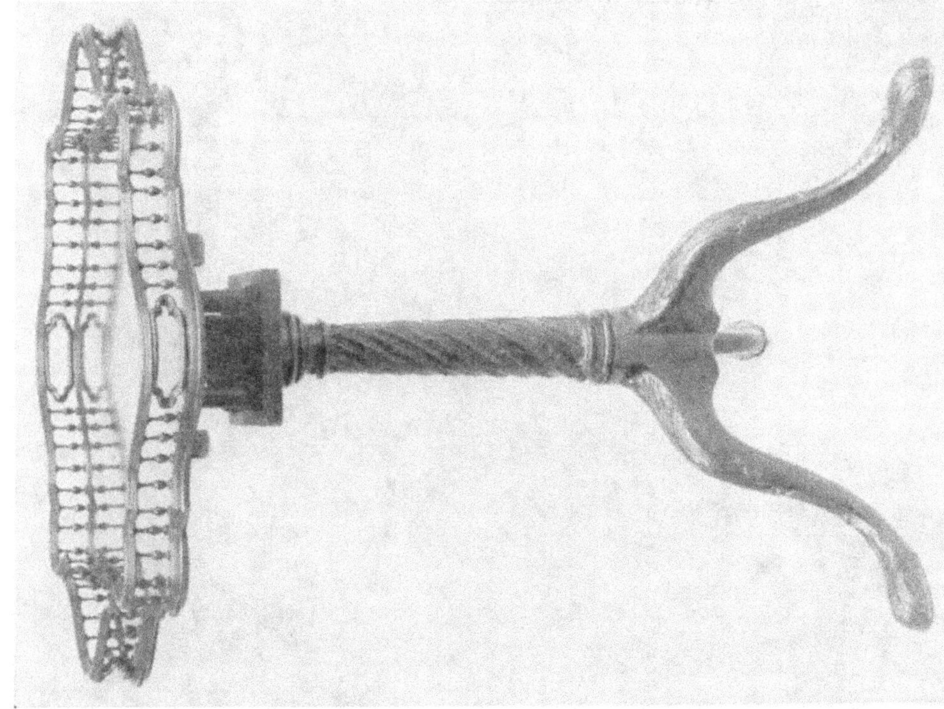

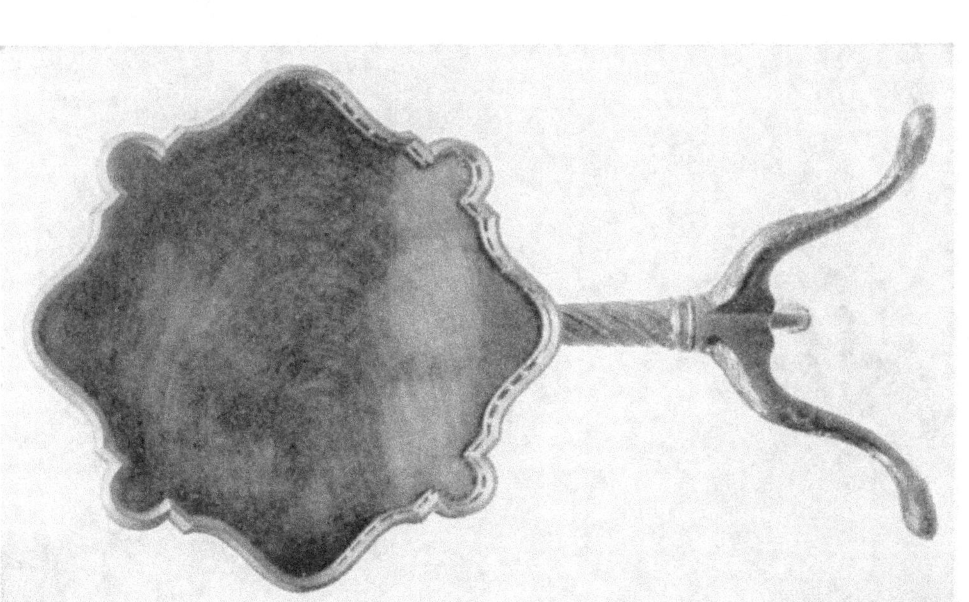

SPIRAL FLUTED PILLAR, ENGLISH, *c. 1760–70.* SPINDLE-GALLERY TOP WITH HAND-HOLES FOR LIFTING

MAHOGANY TRIPOD TABLE

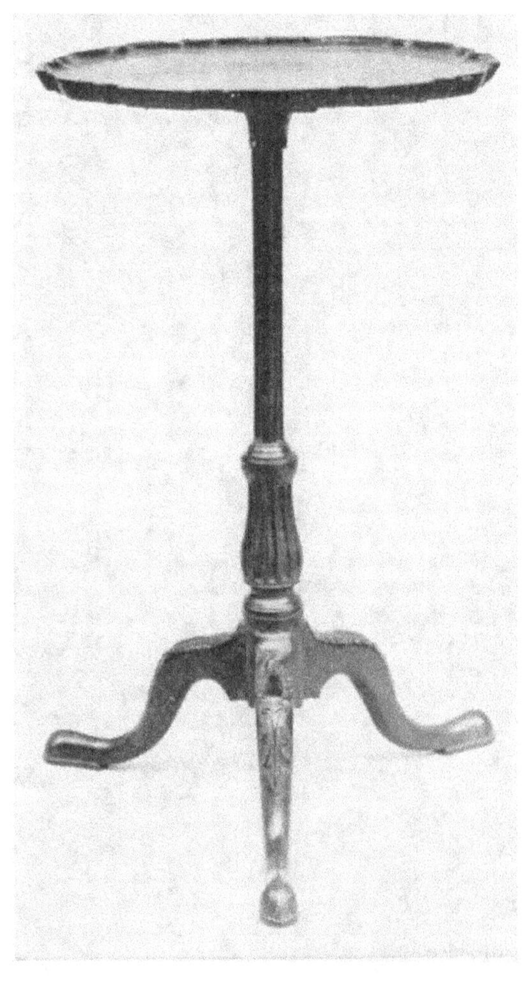

MAHOGANY TRIPOD VASE OR CANDLE STANDS, ENGLISH, *c. 1750*

TRIPOD TABLES OF THE CHIPPENDALE PERIOD

(LEFT) MAHOGANY DUMB-WAITER, ENGLISH, *c. 1760.* CIRCULAR DISHED TOPS, EDGES GADROON CARVED

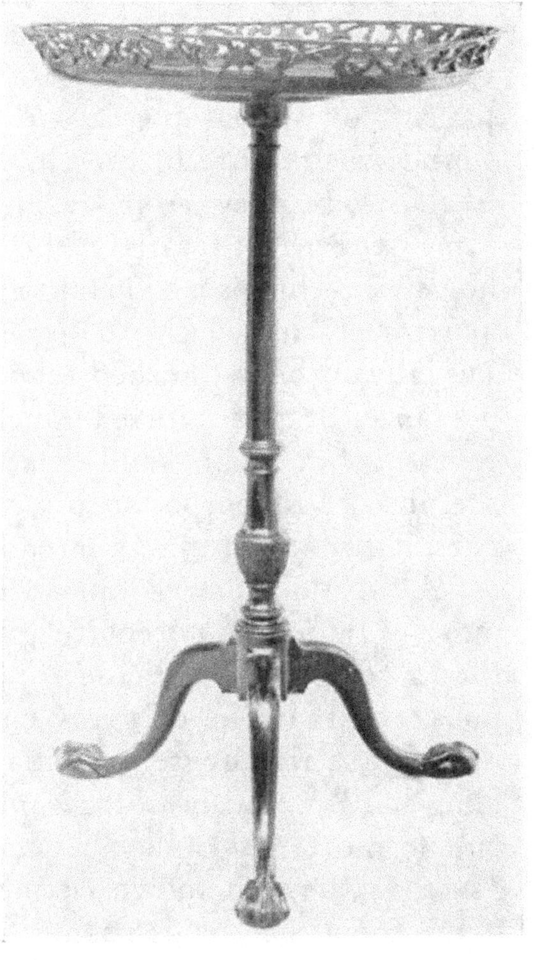

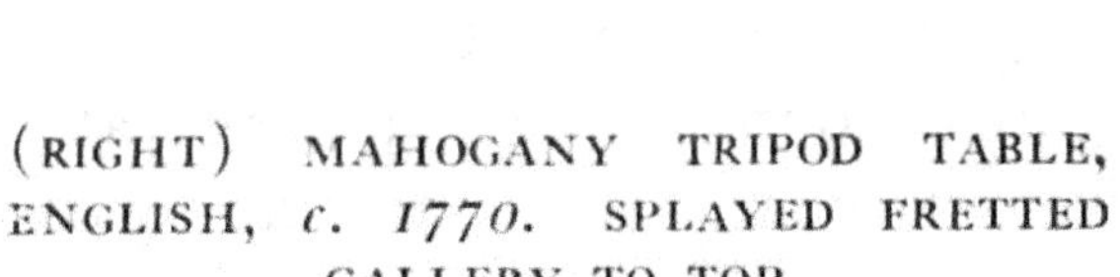

(RIGHT) MAHOGANY TRIPOD TABLE, ENGLISH, *c. 1770.* SPLAYED FRETTED GALLERY TO TOP

TRIPOD TABLES OF THE CHIPPENDALE PERIOD

CHAPTER XII

OCCASIONAL TABLES

PURPOSE-MADE FURNITURE

FASHIONS and habits introduce not only new designs but also new types. Thus, the prevalence of card playing introduces the card table, billiards the billard table, the fashion for afternoon tea, as a function begets the urn table and the tea table. Just as soon as any habit arises, so do furniture types tend to multiply in view of the possible demand. The very paucity of special pieces, prior to the Restoration, shows how simple was the life of the English people, and how free, comparatively, were they from fashionable habits and functions. The same tendency to satisfy the need of the moment still existed, however. Just so soon as the bed room became an important apartment, in which the great lady held her morning *levée,* (usually in bed) the bedstead itself became a piece of huge importance, draped with hangings of silks and velvets, tasseled and fringed with bullion and lace. It is safe to say, therefore, that the absence of purpose-made furniture indicates that the habit or pursuit for which it was intended, did not exist at the time.

A careful consideration of certain pieces will also tell us much more. It does not require great powers of deduction to assert that a tea table was made for an afternoon function in a private house, or that one of great elaboration and costly character was made for a rich house. Similarly, a card table in a club or "gambling hall" would be sturdy and simple; adequate for its purpose, but no more. We may be sure that one with a needlework top, (such as the well-known example at Penshurst) was made, originally, for a rich man's room, and, equally, was never intended for serious card-playing, for high stakes, such as was customary, in fashionable circles, in the latter half of the eighteenth century.

For similar reasons, we can assume that many of the ornate "architects' tables" (of which a notable example is illustrated here) were never intended for professional architects, but for the dilettanti who played at architecture and draughtsmanship. We know that such existed (the Earl of Burlington is a case in point) from the advertisements of teachers of drawing, who always appealed to the "Noblemen and Gentry," of which, possibly, the female element contributed the greater quota to such classes. Had these tables been used professionally, there is doubt that few, if any, would have survived to our day.

CARD TABLES

CARD TABLES were important articles throughout the whole of the eighteenth century. They were made, sometimes in pairs, but more often singly. The folding or hinged top was the rule, generally lined with cloth inside, lipped with an edging of cross-banded veneer. The support for the opened top was variously contrived. Sometimes one only of the back legs swings out on a vertical wooden hinge, occasionally both are hinged. The line of the top framing, by this method, is not continuous, a gap being left by the swung-out leg. A better method, and one usually found in tables of high quality, is where both legs are drawn backward, on a double hinged extension, which is kept rigid by a frame or a slat pulled in grooves provided on the inside of such extensions. When opened, the framing or understructure to the top is continuous, where this method (known as the "concertina-side") is adopted. Both of the back legs must be withdrawn simultaneously, of course.

With the productions of the Hepplewhite school we have three distinct classifications, all of which are illustrated here, the tapered, the turned, and the shaped cabriole, or French leg. With the exception of the turning, and the omission of the square leg, the work of the Chippendale school follows much the same evolutionary course. The French Louis XV manner does not belong to the style of Sheraton or his followers, who preferred to follow that of the next reign.

TEA TABLES

THE tea table, made especially for tea equipage, is more often found in mahogany than in other woods. It is usually oblong, with a slight dishing of the top, and the cabriole was the favorite form of leg. In the Hepplewhite and Sheraton periods the double-flap, or Pembroke table was generally substituted. The Pembroke form is a bridge-piece overlapping the Chippendale and the Hepplewhite, being sometimes found in a manner belonging to the former rather than the latter.

An accompanying piece was the urn table, made to support the silver or plated hot-water urns of the period. The water was heated before being placed in these urns, and kept to a high temperature by a heated cylindrical piece of iron made to fit into a separate casing inside the urn itself, to avoid contact of the iron with the water. A small pull-out slide was provided for the teapot when being filled or refilled. The secret of making tea with water absolutely boiling was unknown at this date, and is far from being general in America at the present day.

Urn tables of the Chippendale period are rare, and nearly always square with outward splayed legs. In the Hepplewhite and Sheraton manners they are sometimes oval or circular. They are among the most dainty of all the pieces which these two periods can show, and both Hepplewhite and Sheraton illustrate examples in the "Guide" and the "Drawing Book," respectively.

ARCHITECT'S OR DRAWING TABLE, ENGLISH, *c. 1760*

MAHOGANY TABLE OF THE CHIPPENDALE PERIOD

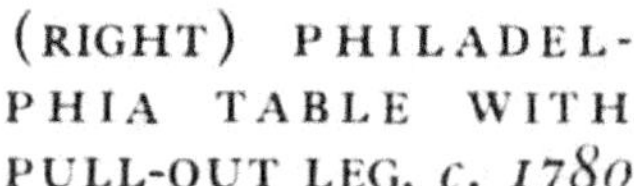

(RIGHT) PHILADELPHIA TABLE WITH PULL-OUT LEG, *c. 1780*

(LEFT) ENGLISH TABLE, WITH HINGED TOP AND PULL-OUT LEG, *c. 1760*

MAHOGANY CARD TABLES OF THE CHIPPENDALE PERIOD

CHIPPENDALE STYLE TABLE WITH FRETTED FRAMING AND CLUSTER-COLUMN LEGS, *c. 1760*

HEPPLEWHITE OR ADAM STYLE TABLE, INLAID WITH STRINGING, *c. 1785–90*

ENGLISH MAHOGANY CARD TABLES

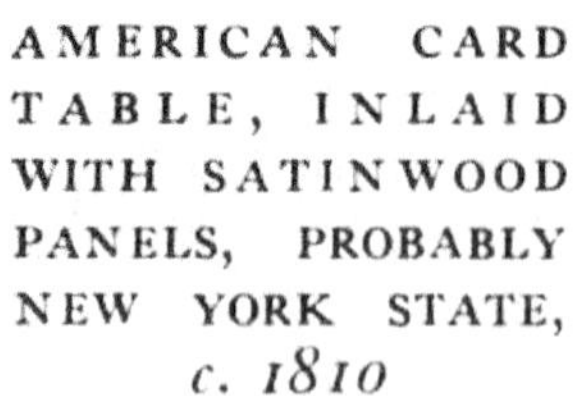
AMERICAN CARD TABLE, INLAID WITH SATINWOOD PANELS, PROBABLY NEW YORK STATE, *c. 1810*

PAIR OF SEGMENTAL SIDE TABLES. MAHOGANY INLAID, *c. 1790*, HEPPLEWHITE

ENGLISH AND AMERICAN MAHOGANY TABLES

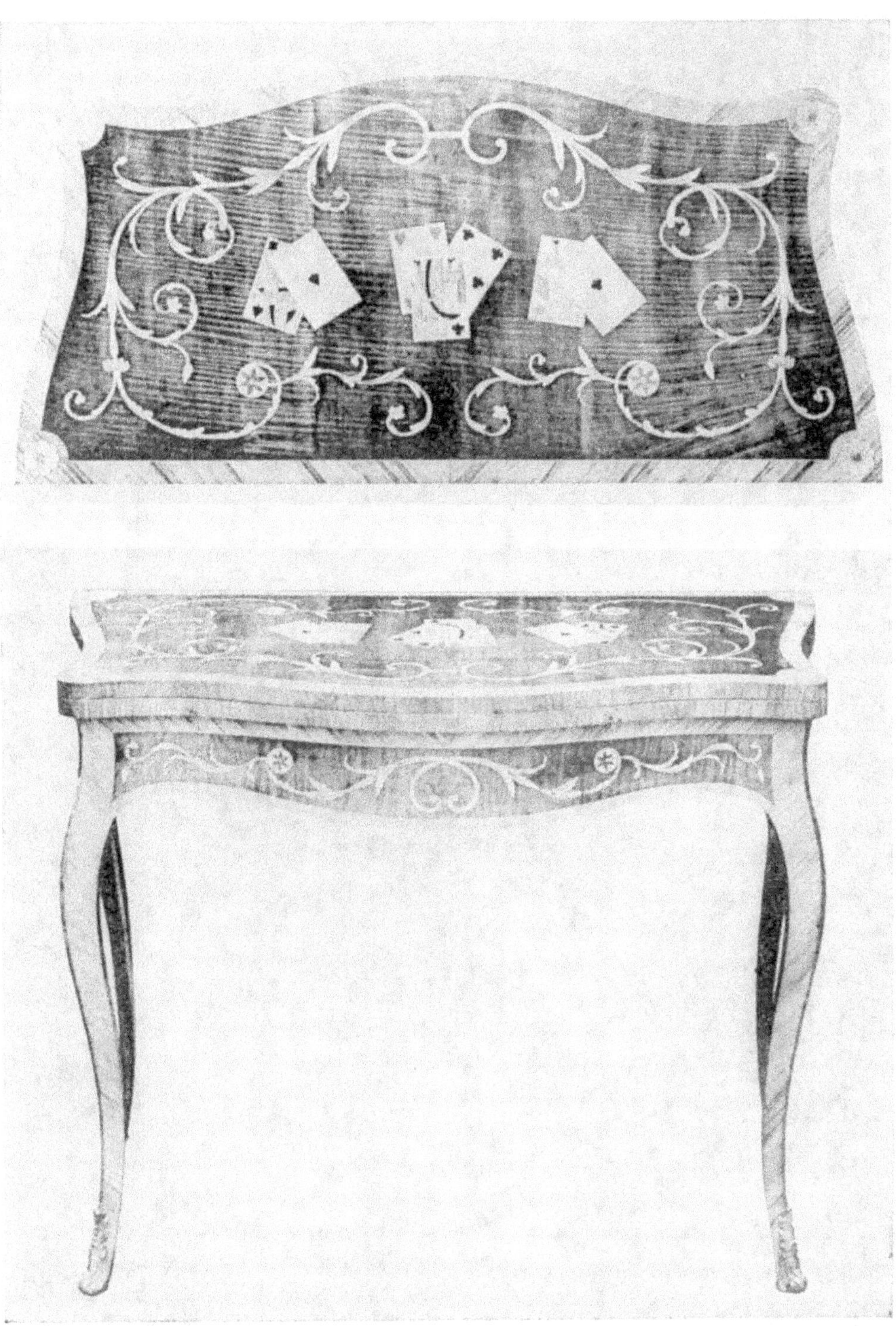

HAREWOOD AND TULIPWOOD, INLAID WITH MARQUETERIE. THE LOUIS XV MANNER OF THE HEPPLEWHITE SCHOOL, *c. 1788–90*

HEPPLEWHITE CARD TABLE

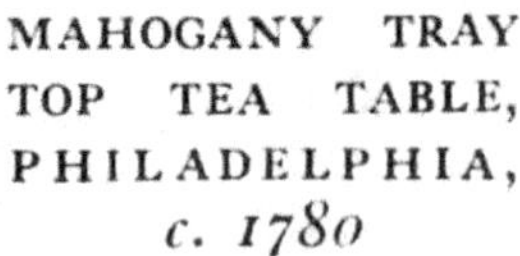

MAHOGANY TRAY TOP TEA TABLE, PHILADELPHIA, *c. 1780*

MAPLE OBLONG TABLE. THE CRUDE NEW ENGLAND TYPE OF *c. 1770*

AMERICAN OCCASIONAL TABLES

MAPLE TEA TABLE, AMERICAN, PROBABLY MARYLAND OR VIRGINIA, *c. 1770–80*

MAHOGANY PEMBROKE TABLE. CLUSTER - COLUMN LEGS. IN THE MANNER OF THE CHIPPENDALE SCHOOL

OCCASIONAL TABLES

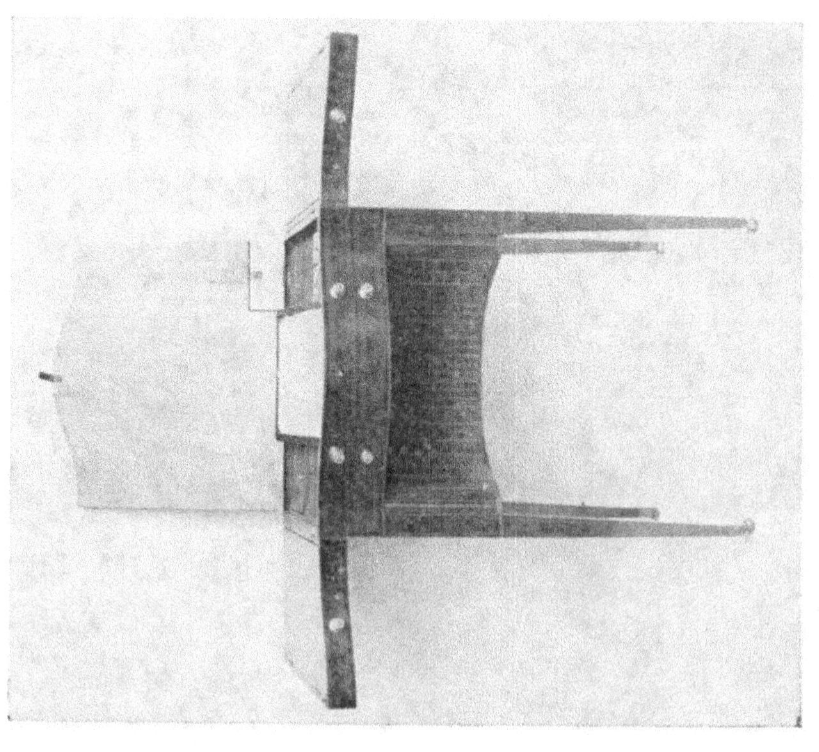

ENCLOSED DRESSING TABLE, *c. 1790–5.* SHERATON STYLE

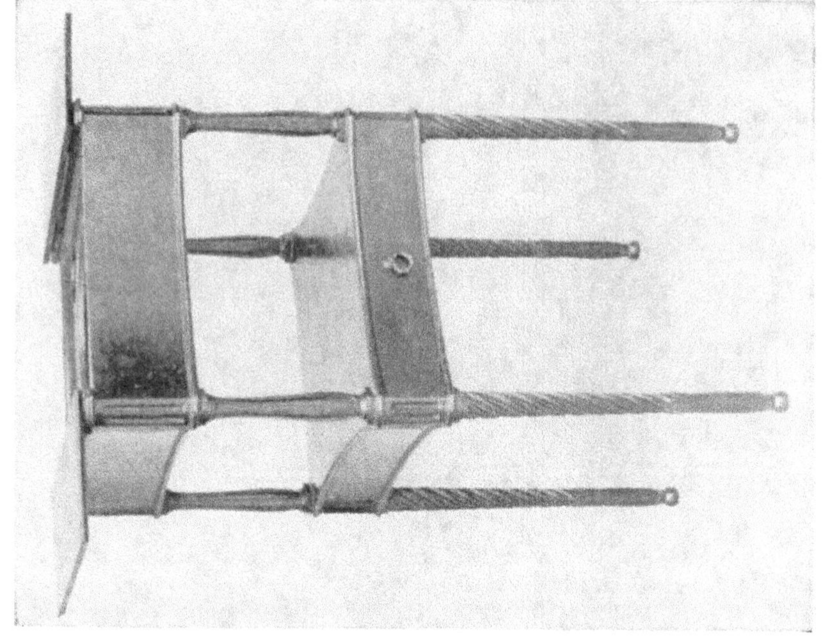

ENCLOSED WASH TABLE, *c. 1795.* SHERATON STYLE

ENGLISH MAHOGANY TOILET TABLES

CHAPTER XIII

WALL FURNITURE OF THE EIGHTEENTH CENTURY

BUREAU FORMS

THE cabinet or bookcase combined with the slant-front bureau belongs more to the Chippendale school than to that of Hepplewhite, whereas the vertical-fronted *secrétaire,* which falls on side quadrants, belongs to the manner of the latter and that of Sheraton which succeed it. These fall-front *secrétaires,* which are only the bureau form thinly disguised, with the front vertical instead of at an angle, are to be found in American pieces almost as frequently as in those of English make. They begin quite early, in the closing years of the seventeenth century, but are improved in the hands of the Sheraton and Hepplewhite schools, by making the entire secretary as a drawer with a hinged front, made to pull out to a certain distance, thereby bringing the inside drawers, cupboards or pigeonholes flush with the front of the piece, instead of being hidden in a cavity, while, at the same time, allowing a greater depth for the writing bed.

Besides the slanted and the vertical fronts, there is a third method which is sometimes (although rarely) adopted, where the top, or shelf to the lower stage, is hinged to unfold forwards, the projecting flap being supported on pull-out slides, or "lopers," in the older bureau fashion. With the vertical secretary, owing to the side quadrants, these "lopers" are dispensed with, an obvious advantage, as the support to the front, when down, is self-acting, whereas the slide may be overlooked, with the result that the hinges are often badly strained.

THE CHINA CABINET AND BOOKCASE

IT IS doubtful whether the china cabinet, enclosed by glazed doors, ever existed in the Chippendale period. Certainly, when Thomas

Chippendale illustrates what he calls a "China Case" in the "Director" it is merely a decorative arrangement of open shelving, what we would know, at the present day, as a hanging bracket or an *étagère*. It is more than probable that china was rarely collected, and the shelves in many of these large cabinets which stand on the floor, and in two horizontal stages, being movable, in lateral grooves, indicate that they were intended for books rather than china or similar pieces. It is not an invariable rule, by any means, for the doors of these bookcases to be glazed; they were often solid-paneled or with glazed lenticles disproportionate in size to the actual door itself. It was an age of good, but not gaudy bindings, although the eighteenth century book is usually sewn on cords, with a flexible back; an honest genuine binding, whereas the present-day "cased" book is a sham, often rendered all the more outrageous by a wealth of "blind" and gilded tooling.

AMERICAN VS. ENGLISH CRAFTSMANSHIP

WHILE much of the American furniture which was made for the great houses of the Early Republican period is fine in workmanship and in the choice of veneers, it could hardly be expected to possess the traditions of the English work. During the whole of the eighteenth century, the sole arbiter, in matters of proportion, was the cabinetmaker, who had little to guide him other than tradition, which is only another name for inherited accuracy in such matters. Many of the published design books exhibit either execrable draughtsmanship, as with Manwaring, or the utter untechnicality of the engraver. It is in this department of careful detailing, coupled with a just sense of proportion, that the sketches of Robert and James Adam are so supreme, yet even the brothers lacked the understanding of material, the consideration of the realization in woods as compared, for example, with plaster, stone, brick or iron. It is here where the English cabinetmakers of the period excelled, in a way in which their American fellow craftsmen could not follow them. Even the finest pieces, those of Philadelphia, are lacking in such particulars; cabriole legs are overcurved and masses are ill-balanced. Goddard and the Newport School are the striking exceptions to this, and even here it is doubtful whether the block-front is a proper detail for execution in wood.

A comparison of the English with the American pieces illustrated in this chapter will show this point very clearly, and neither have been selected with the view of exaggerating the contrast. Had this been the intention, the Philadelphia "Dutch," or German examples could have been selected, which would have over-emphasized the distinction. In point of mere elaboration, the Philadelphia high-boys can hold their own with the English work, and it is somewhat curious that the most ornate furniture of this period was made for the people of the Quaker City, to whom ostentation was supposed to be inhibited.

While on the subject, it may be as well to point out that practically all of the distinctive names used to describe American pieces are of comparatively modern origin. As far as I know, such terms as "high-boy" and "low-boy" are not to be found in any contemporary document, bills, inventories or advertisements. They are useful "tags," but they do not belong to the period of the furniture itself.

MAHOGANY BOOKCASE WITH PAGODA TOP, ENGLISH, CHIPPENDALE, *c. 1760–70.* DOORS AND DRAWERS VENEERED WITH FINELY FIGURED SPANISH MAHOGANY

MAHOGANY BOOKCASE OF THE LATE 18TH CENTURY

MAHOGANY BOOKCASE WITH OVAL LENTICLES IN UPPER DOORS. ENGLISH, *c. 1770–80*. THE CONSTRUCTION OF THIS PIECE IS ONLY POSSIBLE IN ENGLAND. IT WOULD NOT SURVIVE IN AMERICA

MAHOGANY BOOKCASE OF THE LATE 18TH CENTURY

MAHOGANY SECRETARY BOOKCASE, ENGLISH, *c. 1780.* THE LATTICED UPPER DOORS ARE FILLED WITH SOLID PANELS AND THOSE IN THE CENTER ARE PAINTED IN GRISAILLE WITH FIGURES OF FORTITUDE, JUSTICE AND MERCY. SOLD IN THE LEVERHULME SALE IN NEW YORK IN *1926*

MAHOGANY SECRETARY BOOKCASE OF THE LATE 18TH CENTURY

MAHOGANY SECRETARY BOOKCASE, ENGLISH, *c. 1790.* THE DRAWER FRONTS VENEERED WITH FINELY FIGURED AND CENTER-JOINTED CROTCH MAHOGANY

MAHOGANY SECRETARY BOOKCASE OF THE LATE 18TH CENTURY

MAHOGANY AND SATINWOOD SECRETARY BOOKCASE, AMERICAN; PROBABLY NEW YORK, *c. 1800*

MAHOGANY AND SATINWOOD SECRETARY BOOKCASE OF THE LATE 18TH CENTURY

WRITING CABINET OF MAHOGANY, SATINWOOD, TULIPWOOD, ROSEWOOD AND OTHER WOODS. AMERICAN, *c. 1800.* HINGED WRITING FLAP SUPPORTED ON PULL-OUT SLIDES

WRITING CABINET OF THE LATE 18TH CENTURY

MAHOGANY INLAID SECRETARY BOOKCASE, ENGLISH, *c. 1790–1800.* SMALL DRAWERS INSIDE VENEERED WITH CHESTNUT

SECRETARY BOOKCASE OF THE LATE 18TH CENTURY

SECRETARY BOOKCASE OF APPLE AND OTHER WOODS, AMERICAN, NEW ENGLAND, *c. 1820*

SECRETARY BOOKCASE OF THE LATE 18TH CENTURY

HINGED WRITING SLABS SUPPORTED ON PULL-OUT SLIDES; UPPER PARTS ENCLOSED BY SLIDING TAMBOURS, NEW YORK, *c.* 1800

MAHOGANY WRITING CABINETS

HINGED WRITING SLAB, SUPPORTED ON PULL-OUT SLIDES; INLAID WITH FINE HOLLY STRINGING AND INLAID WITH MARQUETERIE. SLIDING TAMBOURS IN UPPER PART, AND CENTRAL DOOR

MAHOGANY WRITING CABINET

MAHOGANY SECRETARY BOOKCASE WITH SCROLLED AND FRETTED PEDIMENT, NEW YORK, *c. 1800*

MAHOGANY BOOKCASE, PROBABLY MARYLAND OR VIRGINIA, *c. 1810–20*

MAHOGANY WRITING CABINETS

CHAPTER XIV

HEPPLEWHITE CHAIRS: ENGLISH AND AMERICAN

HEPPLEWHITE'S "GUIDE"

GEORGE HEPPLEWHITE, cabinetmaker of Cripplegate Ward, in the City of London, died in 1786, and his book, "The Cabinetmaker and Upholsterer's Guide" did not appear, in its first edition, until two years later, issued by his widow, Alice, under the style of "A Hepplewhite & Co." Thomas Chippendale had died in 1779, and the last edition of his "Director" had been published in 1762, so the Hepplewhite style had a clear field.

Unlike the "Director," where the designs were too often unworkmanlike, and certainly not the work of a practical cabinetmaker, those in Hepplewhite's "Guide" are technically accurate, and represent, for its date, a distinctly new style. The school of makers which followed the Hepplewhite traditions (it is obvious that the pieces in this manner, which have survived to our day, are not the work of one man or a single workshop) carried on those of the earlier Chippendale period, especially in wall furniture, and it is often difficult, if not impossible, to postulate where the one style ends and the other begins. In chair models, however, there is a distinct line of demarcation.

CLASSIFICATION OF CHAIR STYLES

THE chair style of the Hepplewhite school may be resolved into several classes, as follows:

(1) The serpentine top rail, with pierced central splats.
(2) The hoop back, also with cut-through central splats.
(3) The shield back, in various forms, either solid, upholstered or with splats or balusters, including the heart-shaped interlaced back.
(4) The oval back, upholstered or splatted.
(5) The kidney-shaped French Louis XV back, usually upholstered.
(6) Various forms or combinations of the above.

The legs of these Hepplewhite chairs are of four kinds: the straight, the tapered (both of these with stretcher-underframing, a revival of the Early Queen Anne traditions), the turned and the cabriole (the two latter borrowed from the Louis XVI and the Louis XV respectively). These are called in the "Guide" "French chairs."

All the above details overlap, in certain models, and mark no progression in the development of the style itself. It is rare to find stretchers in the turned leg chairs, and they never occur in the cabriole form. The seats are either upholstered over the seat rails (the "stitched-up" seat as it is termed) or made loose, to drop into the framing. At one period these were known as "Trafalgar" seats, a name which obviously dates from the early nineteenth century.

AMERICAN HEPPLEWHITE

THE Hepplewhite style permeates the Eastern States of America very thoroughly, and these American chairs are difficult to localize. On the other hand, they are easy to distinguish, especially in the shield-back form, as the shields are nearly always over-large and disproportionate. The American Hepplewhite chair is generally an early nineteenth, rather than a late eighteenth century production, as one would expect, considering how near to the close of the century was the publication of the "Guide." I am inclined to think that the manner was adopted north of the Hudson, in New York and in New England up to Boston; I have never seen a Hepplewhite chair which bore any indications of Pennsylvanian origin, although I have seen others which may have originated in Maryland, Virginia and the Carolinas.

A good deal of the Hepplewhite-Sheraton furniture (the two styles intermingle, especially in America) was made in New York State, principally between New York City and Albany, but it does not appear to have ever appealed to Duncan Phyfe, who seems to have concentrated on the English Empire style.

With the Hepplewhite chair, in its various forms, English chair-work reaches its decorative limit, and the possibilities of construction in wood are exploited to the full extreme. It may be that the return to the square-back of the Sheraton school marks a development towards rationalized design, but the limitations of the latter do not permit the grace and fantasy which is so integral a part of the Hepplewhite style. How great was the reciprocating influence between Hepplewhite and Robert Adam it is difficult to surmise, but the manners of the two definitely overlap, while the designs of the latter steadily improve in practical character, so one can make a reasoned guess.

MAHOGANY HEPPLEWHITE CHAIRS, AMERICAN, *c. 1800.* THE SERPENTINE TOP RAIL AND PIERCED SPLAT; THE CHAIR ON THE LEFT HAS THE PRINCE OF WALES' FEATHER IN THE SPLAT

AMERICAN HEPPLEWHITE CHAIRS

ENGLISH HEPPLEWHITE CHAIR

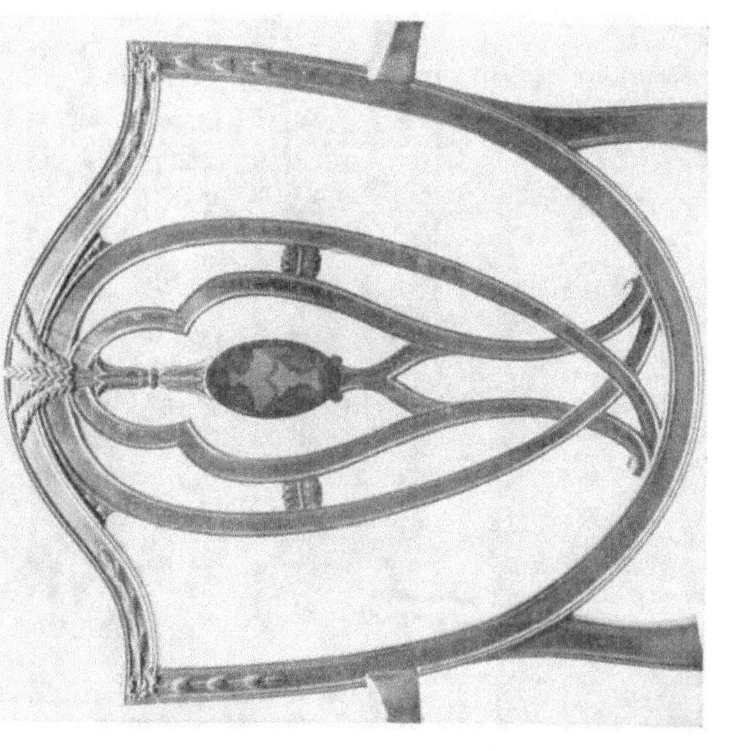

ENLARGED DETAIL OF THE SATINWOOD ARM CHAIR ON THE RIGHT HAND

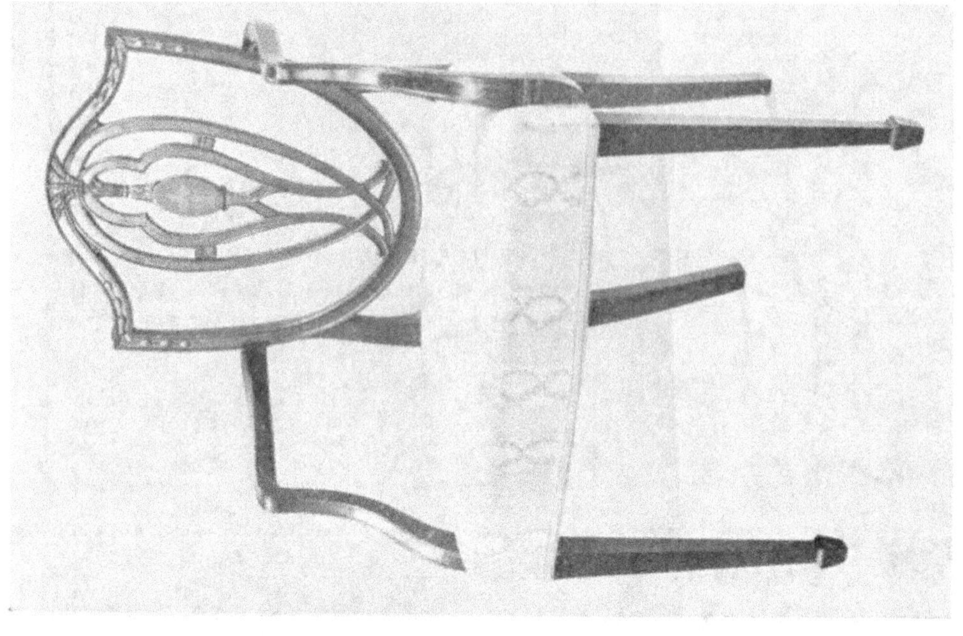

SATINWOOD ARM CHAIR, ENGLISH, *c.* *1785–90.* THE SHIELD BACK OF HEPPLEWHITE WITH CARVED WHEAT-EARS AND INLAID OVAL PANEL IN THE CENTER OF THE SPLAT

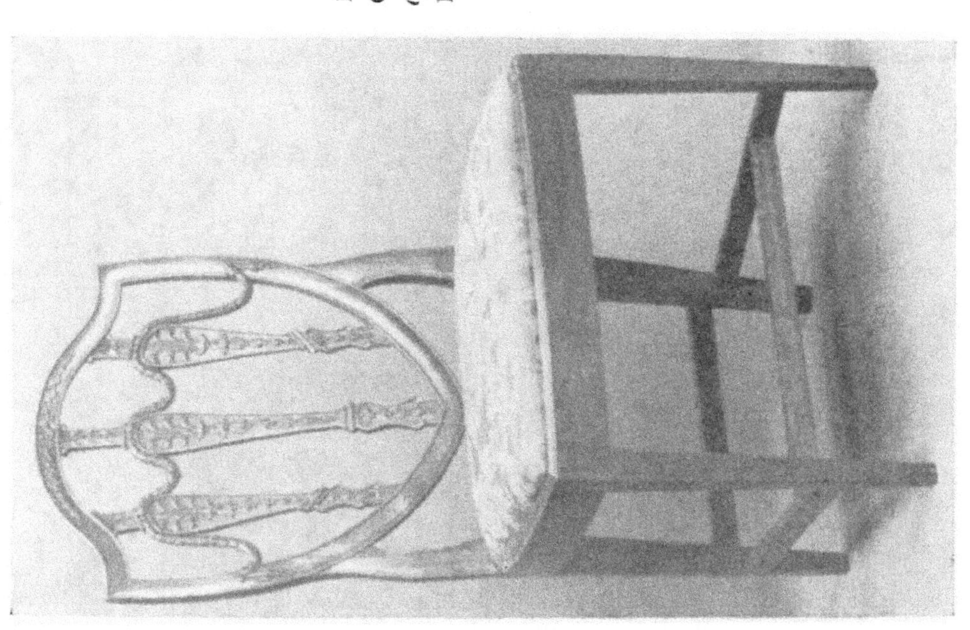

HEPPLEWHITE CHAIRS. ENGLISH, *c. 1785–90.* VARIOUS FORMS OF BACK SPLATTING

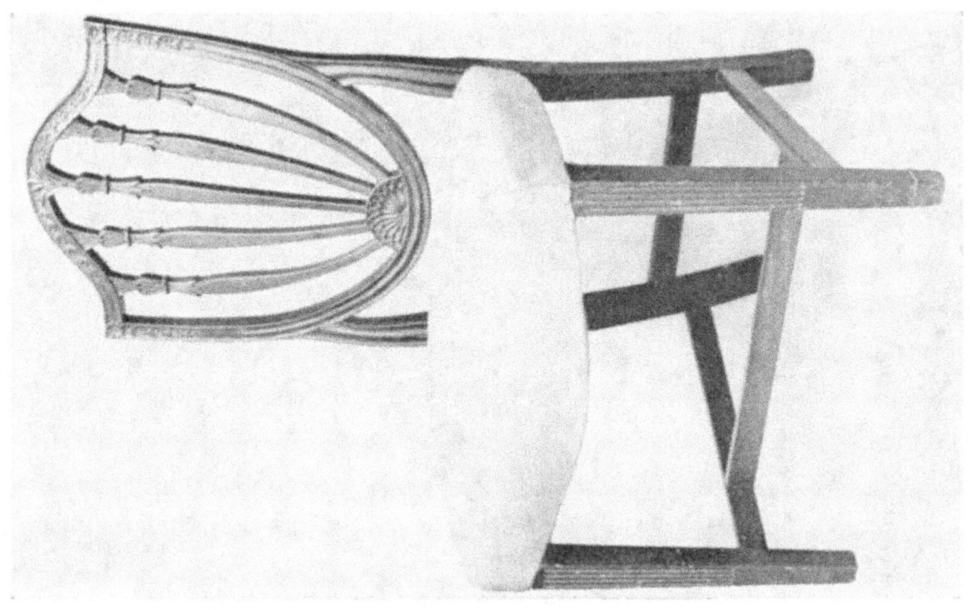

ENGLISH HEPPLEWHITE CHAIRS

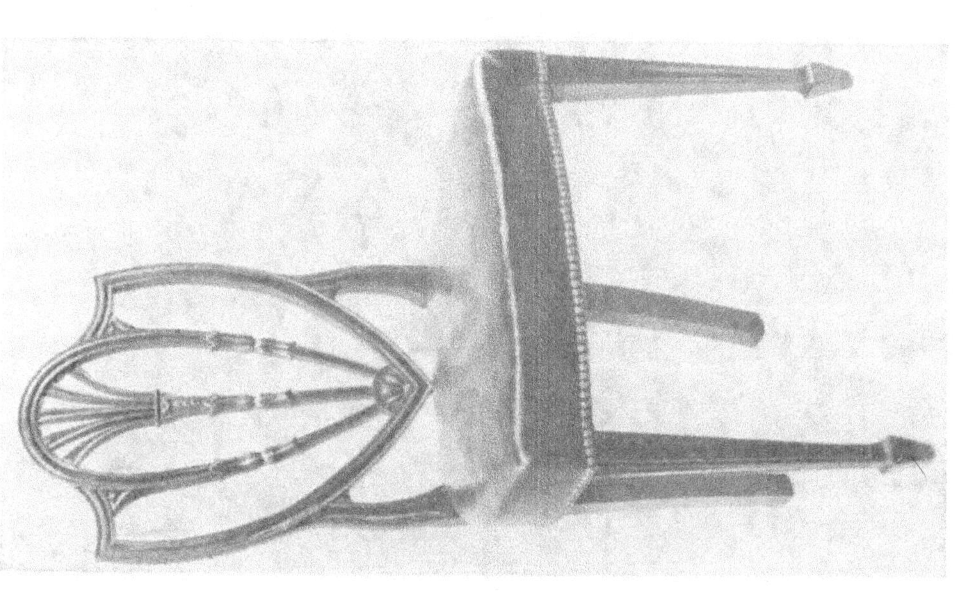

(LEFT) THE INTERLACED HEART-SHAPED BACK

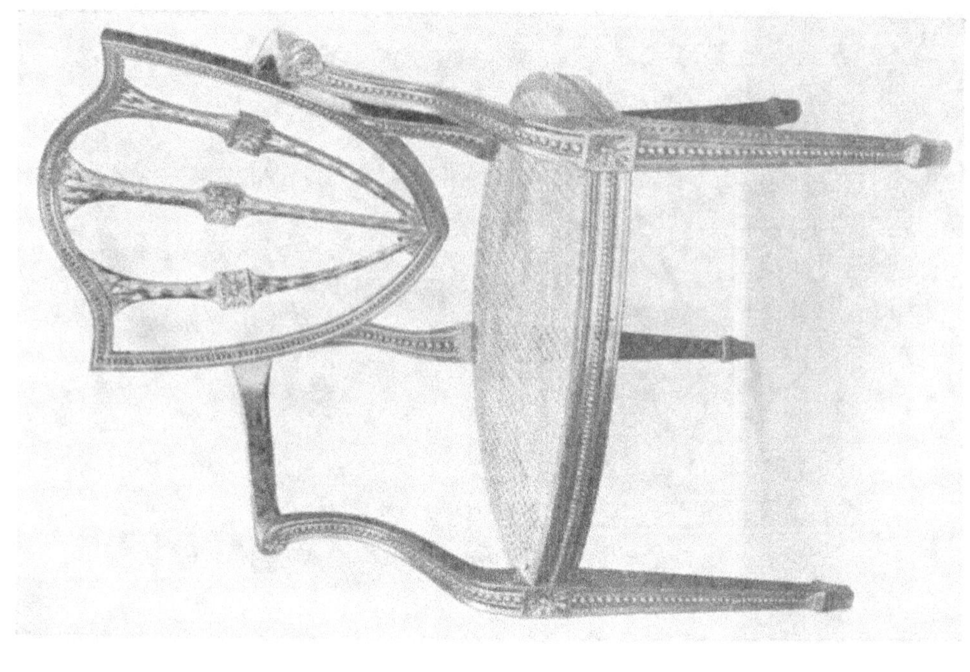

(RIGHT) THE SHIELD BACK WITH CARVED SPLATS

MAHOGANY HEPPLEWHITE CHAIRS, ENGLISH, *c.* 1785–90

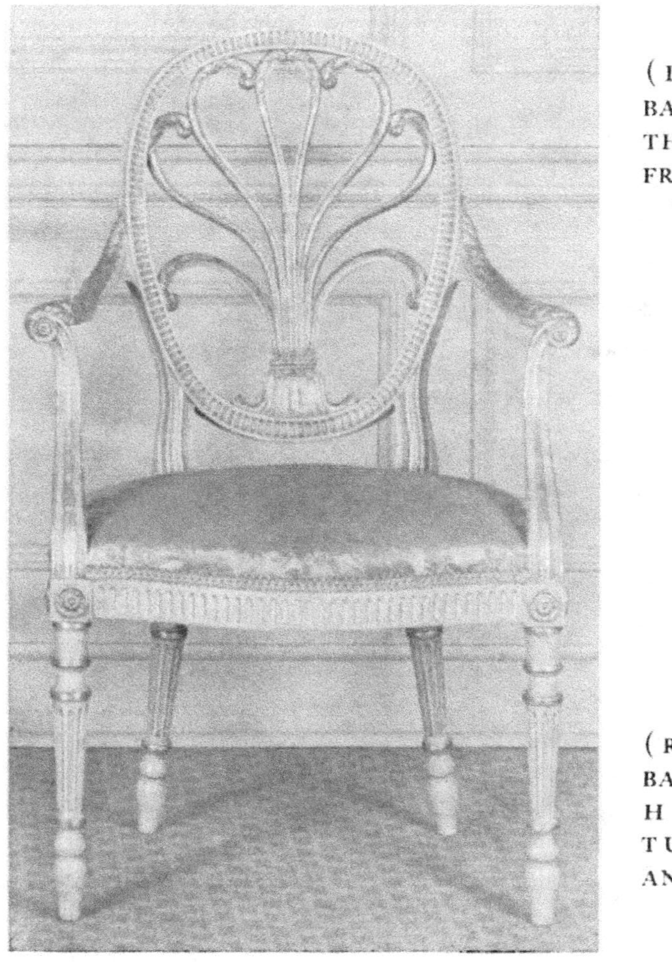

(LEFT) OVAL BACK WITH ANTHEMION SPLAT. FRENCH TYPE OF TURNED LEG

(RIGHT) OVAL BACK SOLID UPHOLSTERED. TURNED LEGS AND STRETCHERS

HEPPLEWHITE CHAIRS, TYPES OF *c*. 1790

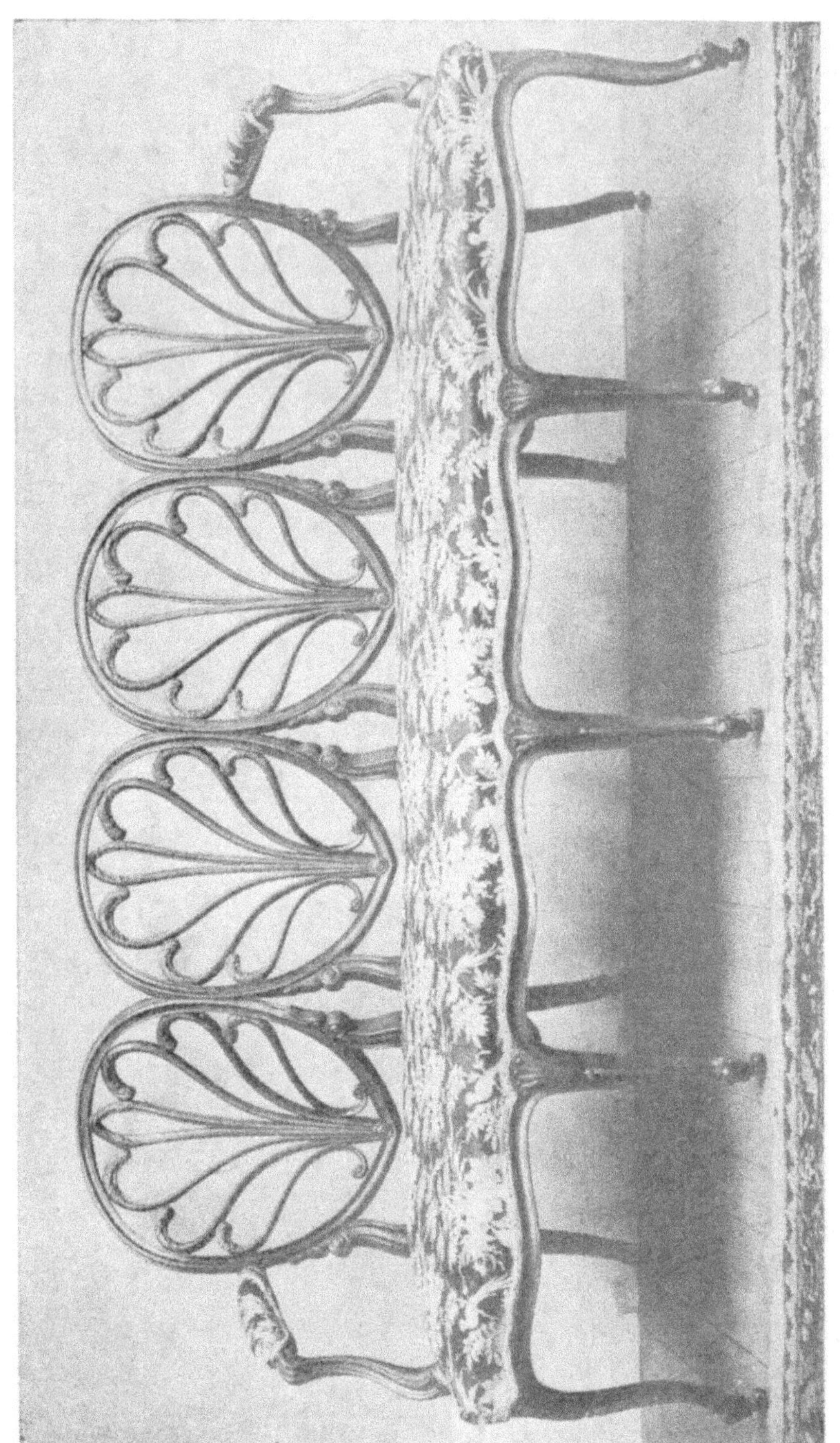

MAHOGANY FOUR-BACK SETTEE, ENGLISH, *c. 1790.* HEPPLEWHITE STYLE. ANTHEMION DECORATION ON BACKS, AND FRENCH CABRIOLE LEGS. IN MANY RESPECTS, A DIRECT COPY FROM THE LOUIS XV

ENGLISH HEPPLEWHITE SETTEE

CHAPTER XV

WALL AND TOILET MIRRORS: AMERICAN AND ENGLISH

GLASS WAS EXPENSIVE

THE cost of glass, whether silvered or plain, was a formidable item of cost throughout the whole of the eighteenth century. Thus, when Thomas Chippendale undertook to make the great pier glasses at Kenwood, Hampstead, on the outskirts of London, for the Earl of Mansfield, the carved and gilded frames are priced at £38, whereas the glass costs £300. It must be remembered that money had more than five times its present-day purchasing value in 1768, but this only increases the figure for the glass in the same ratio. Chippendale, although a successful cabinetmaker, presumably of some financial standing, has to solicit the sum for this glass from the Earl in advance, and he enters into a bond to expend the money in the proper way, and this undertaking has to be endorsed by another cabinetmaker, William France, the obvious inference being that Thomas Chippendale's signature, by itself, was insufficient.

Plain transparent glass was proportionately costly, and one of the items in the expense was the risk of breakage in the manufacture. This danger was enhanced where the glass had to be shaped and worked with an interior bevel, and it was the custom, with large plates, to make them in two or more sections, joined together with a butt-bevel. In France these large plates were seldom attempted, and the mirrors in Versailles, for example, are in many pieces, joined with a metal ribbing.

In the case of prints, of considerable value at the present day, it is difficult to imagine that, at the time when they were new, the glass must have been more costly than the print itself, but those which were framed, at the time when they were issued, nearly always had the broad margins pared down. It is only the prints which were either published in a book, or kept in a portfolio, which have survived to our day with their margins intact.

The greatest difficulty was experienced, in the eighteenth century, in making the glass even and flat, and as the silvering was done by the mercury process, the heavy quicksilver seldom adhered properly to the surface, and was liable to fall off in patches. This accounts for the discolored and opaque appearance of much of this early original silvering. Re-silvering, even by the "patent process" is seldom efficacious; the only method is to regrind the plate on its silvered side. Even then, this is better than replacing the plate with modern glass, as the old has a peculiar greenish-blue tinge which is characteristic and unmistakable, and has a charm which the modern glass does not possess.

EARLY GLASSES

THE early dressing glasses are nearly always of small size, and the cheval glass, of large area, comes into fashion only in the Sheraton period, when costs had become greatly reduced owing to improved processes of manufacture. Wall mirrors of early date, from the latter part of the seventeenth century onwards, even when of larger size, usually have the glass area quite small, being surrounded by broad margins of wood, plain, inlaid, or carved, or of needlepoint or stump-work. These "stump" mirrors of the late Stuart period are among the most characteristic examples of English furniture extant, and as the art of the needle implies a greatly-leisured female class, one would hardly expect to find any American examples of this period.

The early Georgian wall mirrors, of mahogany or walnut, with carved and gilt surround and inside enrichment, were extensively copied in America, and so faithfully that it is often extremely difficult to distinguish between the work of the Eastern States and the English originals, especially when, in the latter, the frame was surmounted by an eagle. These mirrors, both in England and America, were often made in balancing pairs, similar to the two examples shown here.

There is one distinguishing detail which may be pointed out with advantage. With the English mirror, the backboard was cut inside the framing, and beaded from behind, whereas, with the American, the usual custom was to make the backboard larger than the opening, and to nail it to the frame. The result was a space between the backboard and the silvered face of the glass, which, in preventing condensation or abrasion, was the better method, calculated to preserve the silvering for a greater length of time. Perhaps the American craftsmen learned by experience.

TOILET GLASSES AND DRESSING TABLES

THE dressing, or toilet glass, both in England and in America, was rather a small piece, until almost the close of the eighteenth century, a framed mirror, pivoted on standards fixed on a box plateau with drawers. Occasionally these standards were stretchered and placed on "cheval" feet, in the manner of a fire screen, the box and drawers being omitted. Of the former kind, rare examples can be found in walnut, of Queen Anne days, the box plateau having a slant front similar to that on a bureau, and supported on the same pull-out slides. These early dressing glasses are very charming, the mirror framing having usually a delicately shaped head, and the glass a characteristically flat bevel. Toilet mirrors of any kind are conspicuously rare in the Chippendale period, but are plentiful in the styles of Hepplewhite and Sheraton. The Chippendale dressing table was usually an enclosed piece, serving many purposes, with two boxed lids opening sideways, below which were powder and patch boxes and a hinged framed mirror with a strutted back, to support it at any angle. The same method was adopted for the fitting of the top drawer in a chest of drawers, of which type, examples are not uncommon.

During the last ten years of the eighteenth century, the complete dressing table, with an attached swing mirror, came into fashion, being copied in America at a somewhat later date. In these pieces the fashion of the Sheraton school is carried right into that of the succeeding vogue, the so-called English Empire, without any serious modification of the former style. In these dressing tables only, the Sheraton style remains in favor almost throughout the whole of the nineteenth century. It is eminently suitable for pieces of this kind, which may account for the esteem in which it was held.

MAHOGANY AND GOLD WALL MIRRORS, *c. 1770.* NOTE THE SIMILARITY BETWEEN THE TWO, INDICATING A COMMON ORIGIN

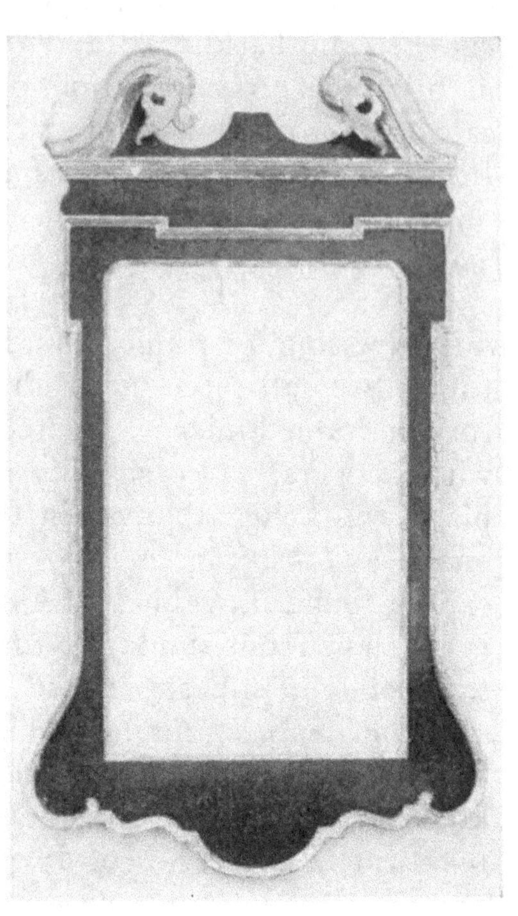

AMERICAN WALL MIRRORS

MAHOGANY AND GOLD WALL MIRRORS, *c. 1780.*
NEW YORK OR PENNSYLVANIA ORIGIN

AMERICAN WALL MIRRORS

COMPOSITION AND GILT MIRRORS. THE PAINTING OF SHIPPING SCENES ON THE UPPER PANELS WAS A USUAL FEATURE. EARLY *19*TH CENTURY

DELICATELY CARVED WALL MIRROR, *c. 1770*. FROM THE MARMION ROOM, NOW AT THE METROPOLITAN MUSEUM OF ART

AMERICAN MANTEL GLASSES

MAHOGANY INLAID TOILET MIRRORS ON BOX PLATEAU STANDS, *c. 1790–1800.* NEW YORK OR NEW ENGLAND

AMERICAN TOILET MIRRORS

MAHOGANY AND MAPLE DRESSING TABLE. SWING MIRROR ON BOX PLATEAU, WITH DRAWERS. NEW YORK STATE, EARLY *19*TH CENTURY

AMERICAN TOILET TABLE WITH MIRROR

CHAPTER XVI

THOMAS SHERATON AND DUNCAN PHYFE

SHERATON AND PHYFE COMPARED

IN THIS closing chapter we are concerned with the work of two men who were widely different, yet had much in common. The family of Phyfe came not far from Inverness, in the extreme north of Scotland, emigrating, while Duncan was only a boy, to America, settling first at Albany, coming down the Hudson, later to lower New York into what is now the Fulton Street and Broadway district.

Thomas Sheraton hailed from farther south, almost on the borders of England and Scotland, being a native of Stockton-on-Tees in County Durham. He was already well advanced in life when he left his home city to seek fame and fortune in London. The latter he was never destined to achieve, his life in the metropolis being spent in poverty and disappointment. His two books, which concern us here, were "The Cabinetmaker and Upholsterer's Drawing Book" and "The Cabinet Dictionary." The former represents the true style which we now know as Sheraton, the latter being in the later and inferior manner, the so-called English Empire, which Sheraton was forced to adopt. It is in this English Empire where Sheraton was undoubtedly the teacher of Duncan Phyfe, although his own style was also extensively followed in New York State by the cabinetmakers of the early nineteenth century.

Sheraton was a trained cabinetmaker (and his designs are always severely practical, in consequence) and in this particular he was the fellow craftsman with Phyfe, but he was also a designer, which Phyfe was not. On the other hand, there is evidence to show that Sheraton never followed his trade during his London life, gaining his living (and a very poor one at that) as a teacher of drawing, a publisher of books, and an itinerant preacher of Baptist doctrines.

HEPPLEWHITE AND SHERATON

BOTH Hepplewhite and Sheraton borrowed from French sources, but the former was the more catholic, adapting from the Louis XV and the Louis XVI styles indifferently. The latter preferred the restrained simplicity of the Louis XVI style, with the square back and the turned leg to chairs, and, in these details, Sheraton is distinct in his style, whereas in sideboards, tables, and similar pieces, there is very little, if any, line of demarcation between the Hepplewhite and the Sheraton. The latter also did influence the trade of his time, both in England and America, and had something new to offer to the cabinet trade, whereas it is more than probable that the former merely consolidated the patterns of the trade of his time, giving them artistic permanence in book form. Hepplewhite was a practising cabinetmaker, which Sheraton was not, and he died in 1786, two years before his "Guide" was published. Sheraton, on the other hand, saw three editions of the "Drawing Book" through the press, altering, improving and adding with each succeeding issue.

OUTLINE OF SHERATON'S LIFE

THOMAS SHERATON was born in Stockton-on-Tees in 1750, but he was already in his fortieth year when he came to London. He had projected, if not completed, his "Drawing Book" before he left County Durham, and his list of subscribers seems to show that he obtained many of these by personal canvass, probably making his long journey in stages, very likely on foot. The first edition appeared in London in 1791, the second in 1793 and the third in 1802. For the first he obtained 522 subscribers in all. "The Cabinet Dictionary" appeared in 1803 and in the following year he issued the first, and only part of an ambitious publication, projected in 125 folio numbers, entitled "The Cabinetmaker's, Upholsterer's and General Artist's Encyclopædia," but he died on October 2nd, 1806 with the undertaking unfulfilled. The "Little Corporal" was leaving his mark on Europe at this period, and the time was unpropitious for large publishing ventures concerned with the arts of peace.

PHYFE'S LIFE

DUNCAN PHYFE had the typical solidity of the Scot. He learned his trade in his father's shop in Albany as a boy of sixteen, and later on came to New York and established himself first at Broad Street, and afterwards at 35 Partition Street (now that part of Fulton Street which lies west of Broadway), making fine furniture in the English Empire style of Sheraton and Thomas Hope, where his craftsmanship and selected lumber earned him considerable renown among the wealthy of the city of that day. In 1795 Partition Street was re-christened Fair Street, a fact which has led some writers astray as indicating a removal instead of the renaming of a street.

In 1837 the firm was called "D. Phyfe & Sons" and in 1840 "D. Phyfe & Son," which seems to indicate the death of one of the sons, but there is no exact record of this. In 1847 the elder Phyfe retired, and lived at 193 Fulton Street (east of Broadway) until his death in 1854. He was buried in Greenwood Cemetery, Brooklyn. Born in 1768, in Loch Fannick, near Inverness, Scotland, he came to America in his fifteenth year, and lived to the ripe age of eighty-six.

So much of this American-made mahogany furniture in the English Empire manner has been labeled "Duncan Phyfe" on the mere style-resemblance, that in justice to Phyfe, it must be pointed out the mere style is no criterion whatsoever. Phyfe's choice of fine mahogany, and the manner of his carving (the latter possibly dictated by the extreme hardness of the former) are unmistakable when one has made a study of authentic examples, and what little I have succeeded in mastering of this subject I owe to that painstaking student, and ardent collector of Phyfe's work, R. T. Haines Halsey of New York City, whose knowledge is surpassed only by his modesty. I wish he had been available to write this chapter, while I was engaged on this book.

CONTEMPORARIES

If Phyfe was no original designer, Sheraton was no cabinetmaker during his fifteen years of life in London. There is another designer-cabinetmaker who has been too much neglected, as he was, possibly, the creator of what we know as the "Sheraton style." This was Thomas Shearer, whose "Designs for Household Furniture" appeared in 1788, three years before Sheraton's "Drawing Book." Shearer had only a small shop, but he did make furniture in London, and many of the so-called "Sheraton" pieces may be Shearer's work. Another notable firm was Seddon, Sons and Shackleton, of Aldersgate Street in the City of London, who had an establishment of considerable size, and much of Robert Adam's fine furniture came from this factory. But for the accident that they neglected to publish a trade catalogue or book of designs (the two were often synonymous) we might have a "Seddon style" at the present day, with far greater reason, in actual work realized in wood, than a "Chippendale," a "Hepplewhite" or a "Sheraton," which shows the mistakes which one makes in neglecting to consider posterity.

PAINTED ARM CHAIR, ENGLISH, *c. 1795*, SHERATON. TOP HAND-RAIL WITH CANED PANEL BELOW

MAHOGANY SIDE CHAIR, ENGLISH, *c. 1800*. TOP HAND-RAIL, WITH INLAID PANEL IN CENTER

ARM AND SIDE CHAIRS, *c.* 1795, 1800

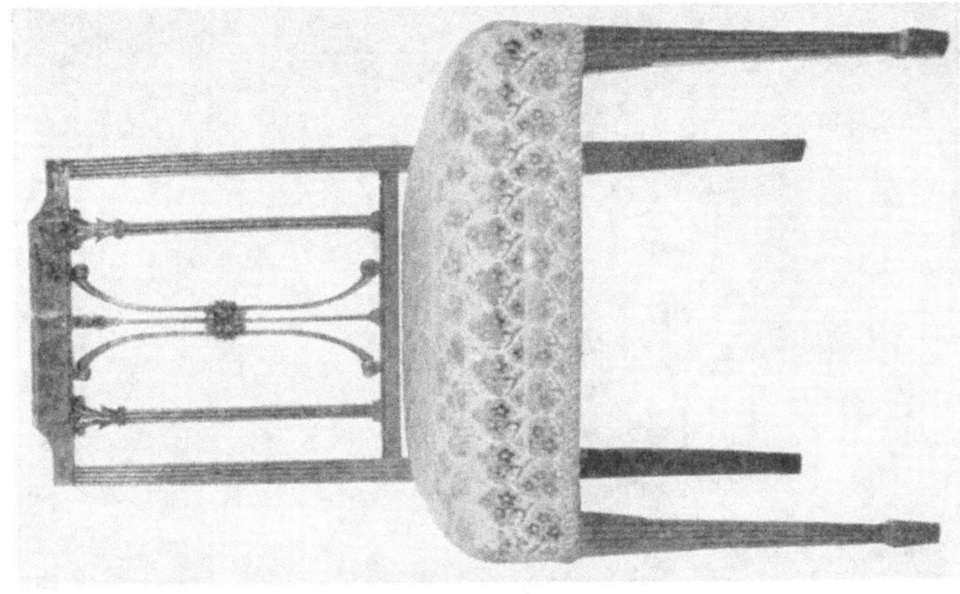

MAHOGANY CHAIRS IN THE SHERATON STYLE, AMERICAN, *c. 1810.* THE TYPICAL SHERATON SQUARE BACK

MAHOGANY CHAIRS IN THE SHERATON STYLE

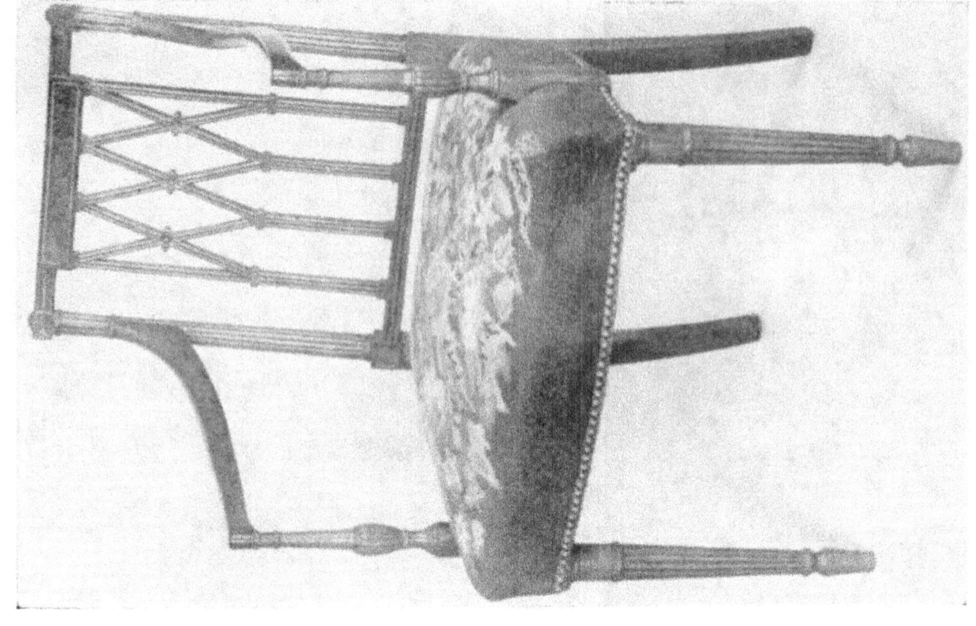

SHERATON STYLE CHAIRS OF *c. 1795*

(LEFT) SQUARE BACK WITH PIERCED VASE

(RIGHT) SQUARE BACK LATTICED

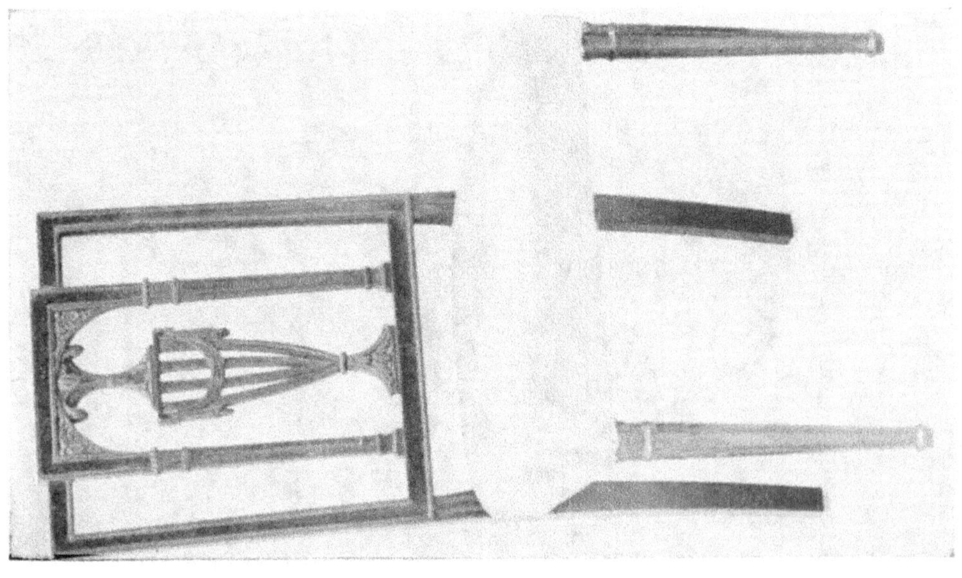

SQUARE-BACK AND LATTICE-BACK SHERATON CHAIRS

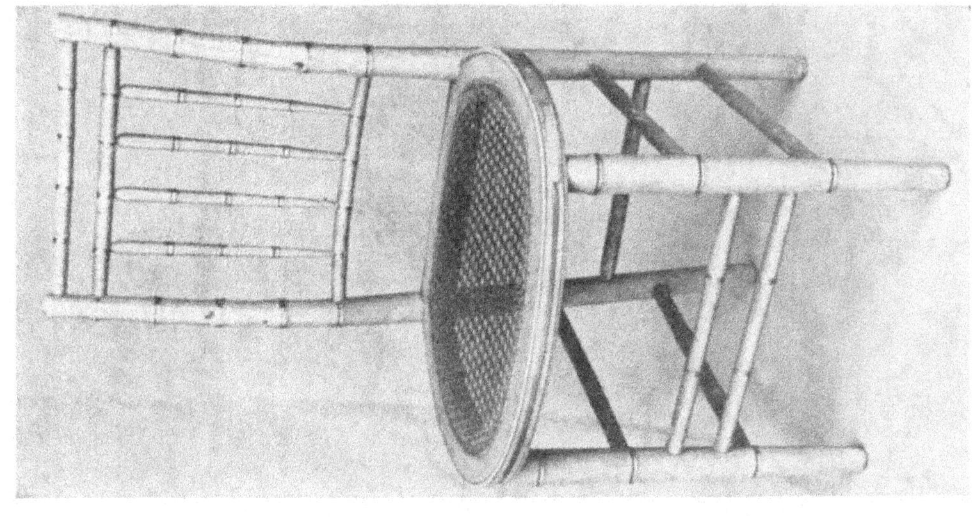

THE CRAZE FOR THE IMITATION OF BAMBOO IN WOOD. PAINTED CHAIRS IN THE SHERATON MANNER OF *c. 1800*

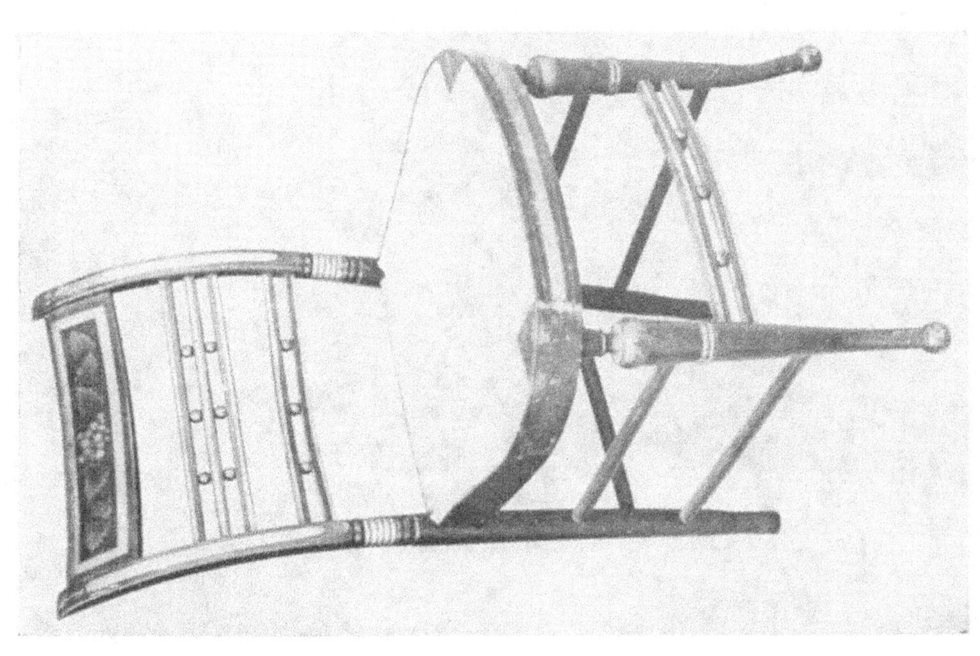

CHAIRS IMITATING BAMBOO IN THE SHERATON STYLE

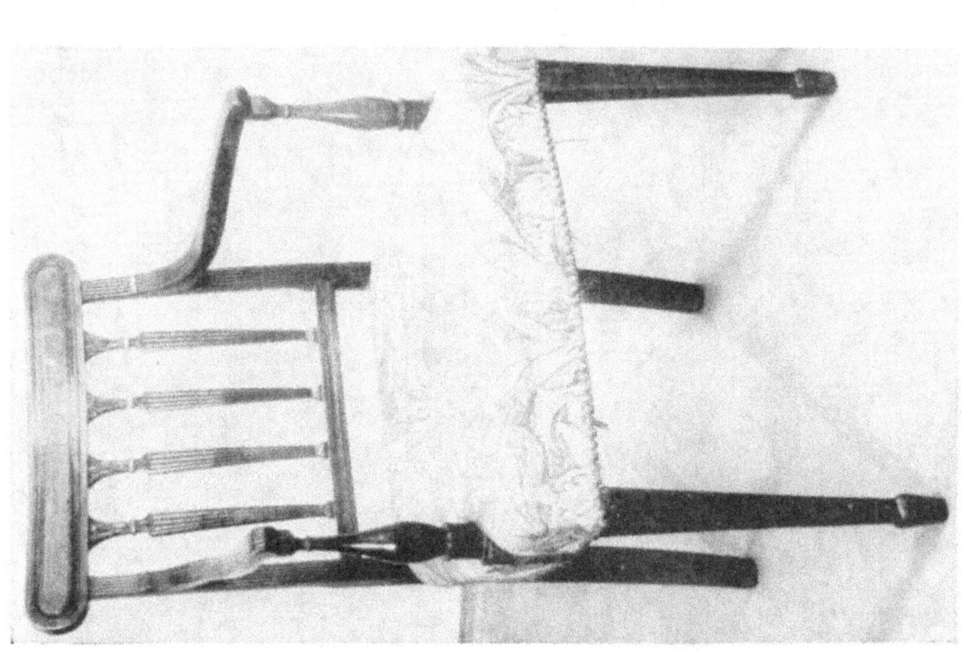

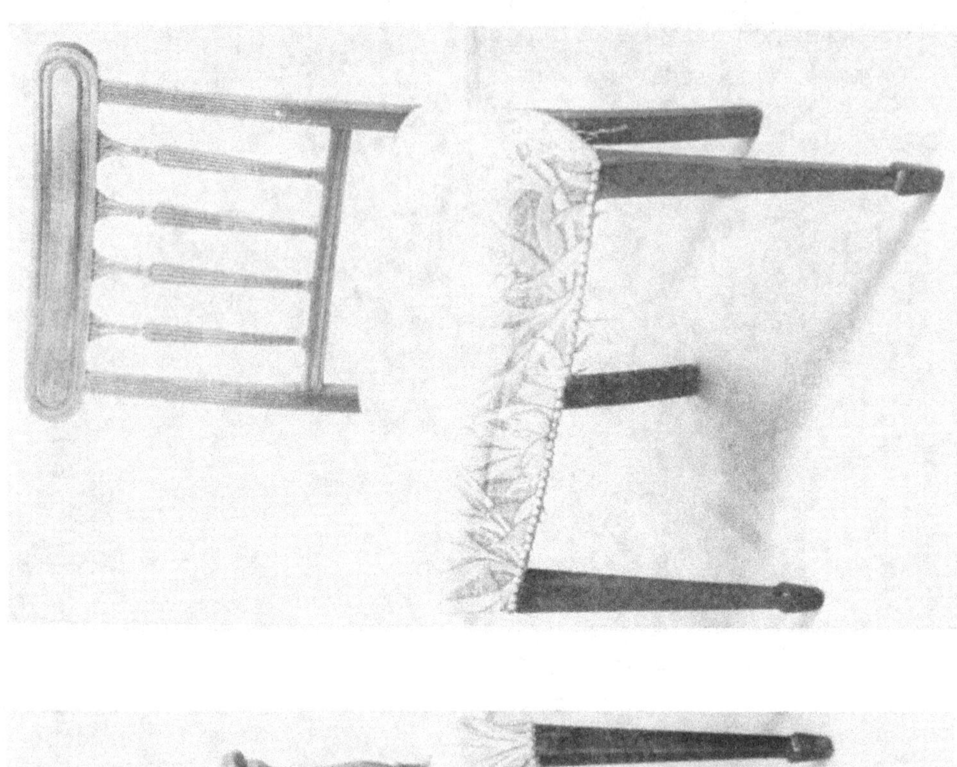

MAHOGANY ARM AND SIDE CHAIRS, ENGLISH, *c.* *1800*. THE BRIDGE FROM THE SHERATON TO THE ENGLISH EMPIRE

MAHOGANY CHAIRS TRANSITIONAL FROM SHERATON TO EMPIRE

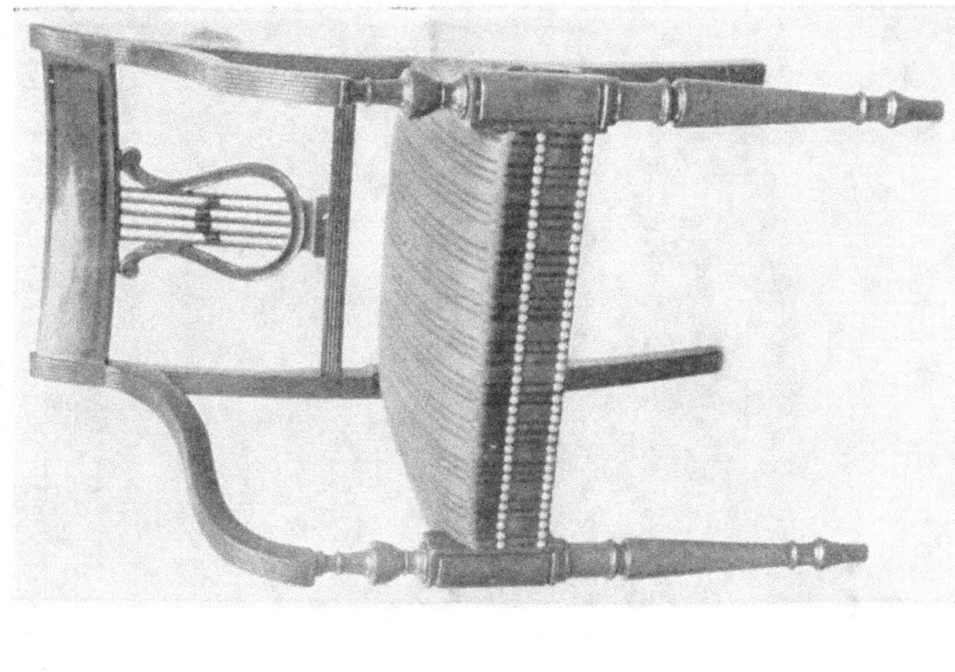

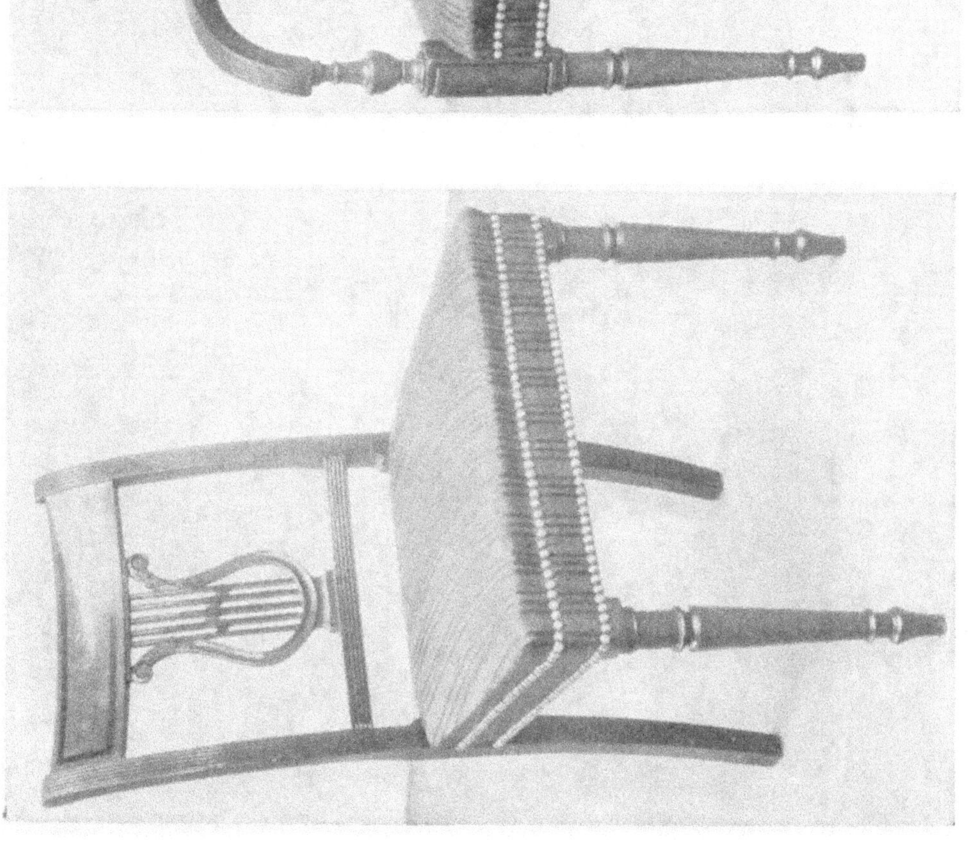

MAHOGANY ARM AND SIDE CHAIRS, ENGLISH, *c. 1810.* THE LYRE SPLAT AND THE TURNED FRONT LEG

MAHOGANY CHAIRS WITH LYRE SPLAT AND TURNED FRONT LEGS

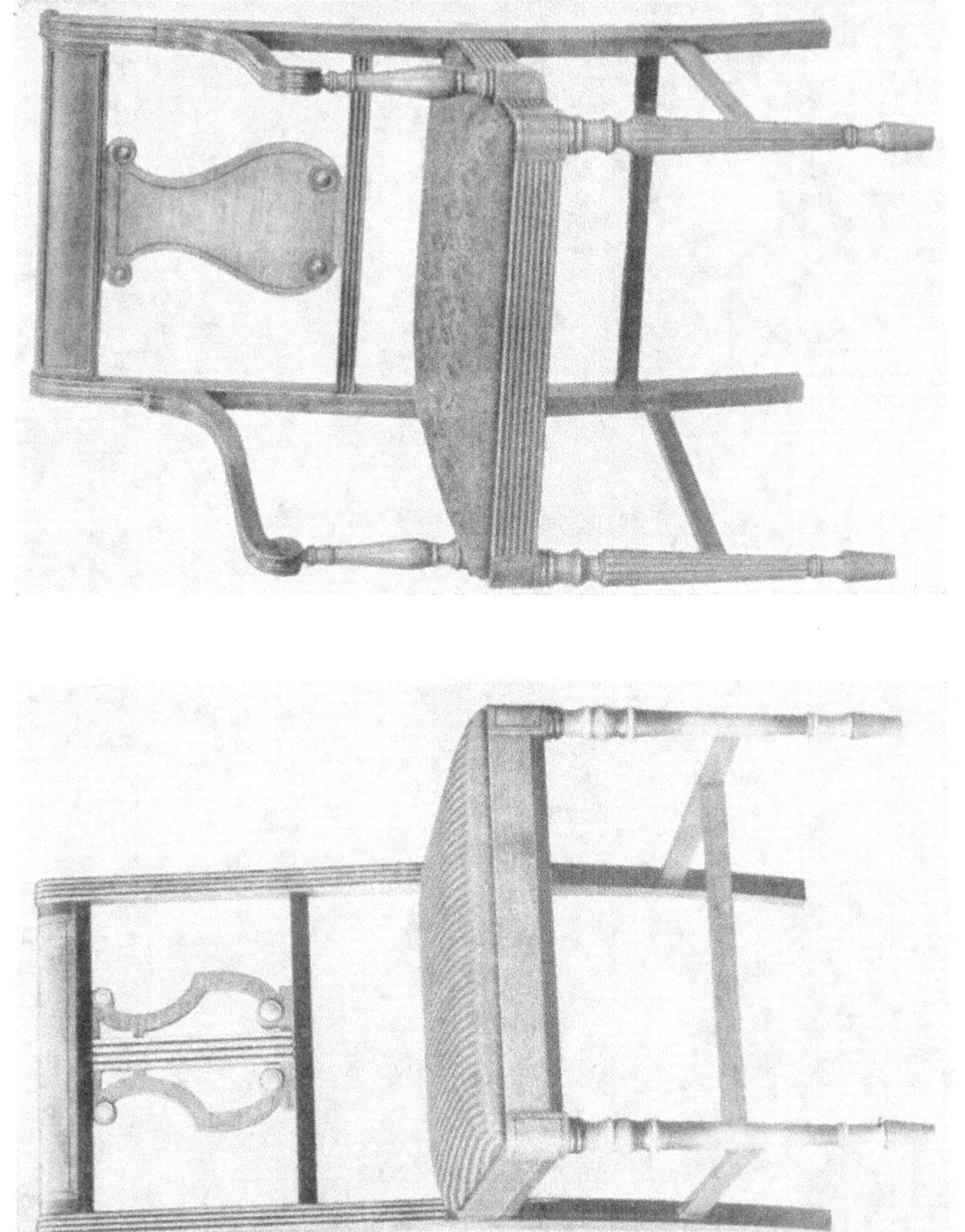

MAPLE CHAIRS, AMERICAN. NEW ENGLAND VERSION OF THE PHYFE MANNER. THE LYRE SPLAT AND TURNED FRONT LEG

CHAIRS IN THE NEW ENGLAND VERSION OF THE PHYFE MANNER

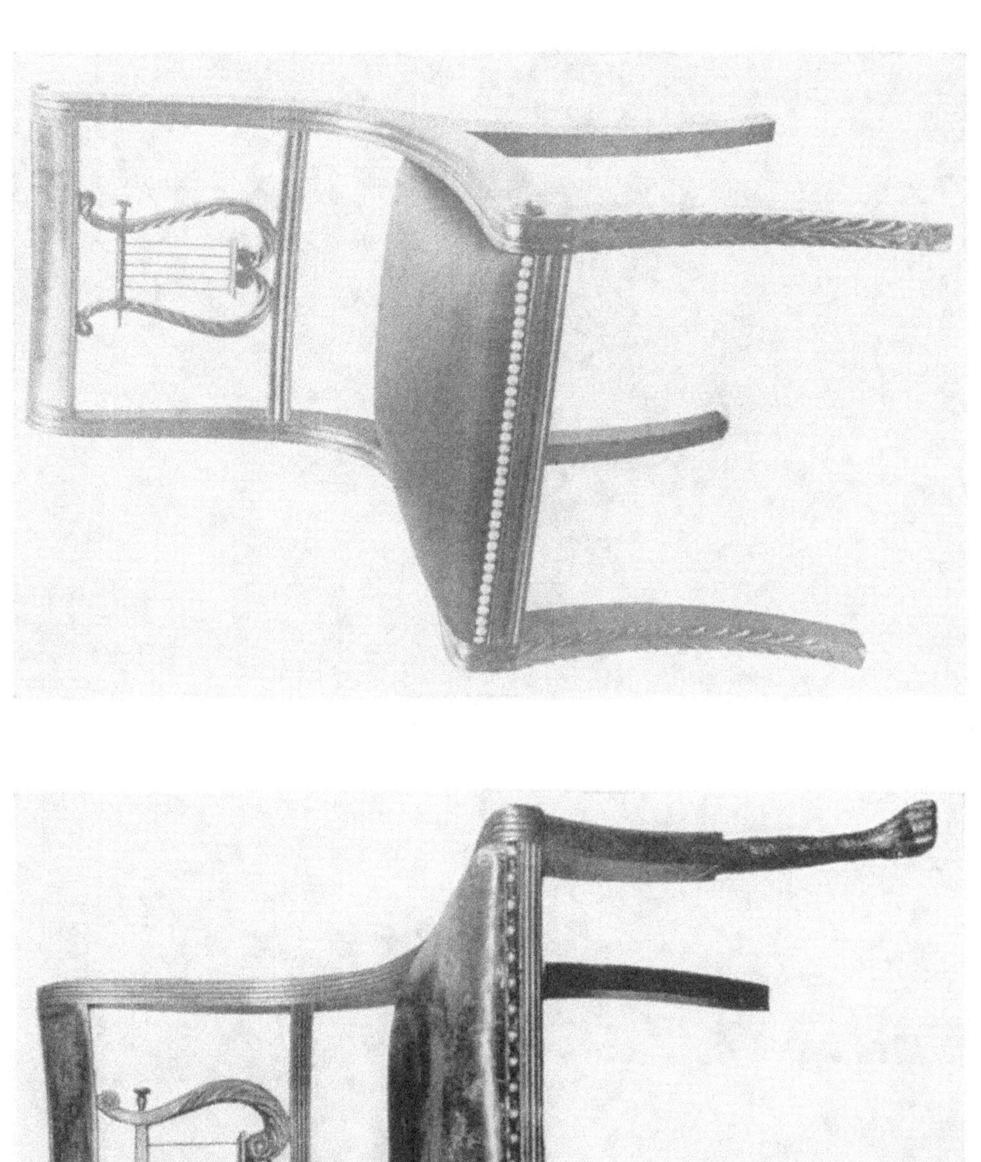

MAHOGANY SIDE CHAIRS, AMERICAN, STYLE OF DUNCAN PHYFE. EARLY *19TH* CENTURY. THE LYRE SPLAT AND INCURVING FRONT LEGS

MAHOGANY CHAIRS OF DUNCAN PHYFE STYLE

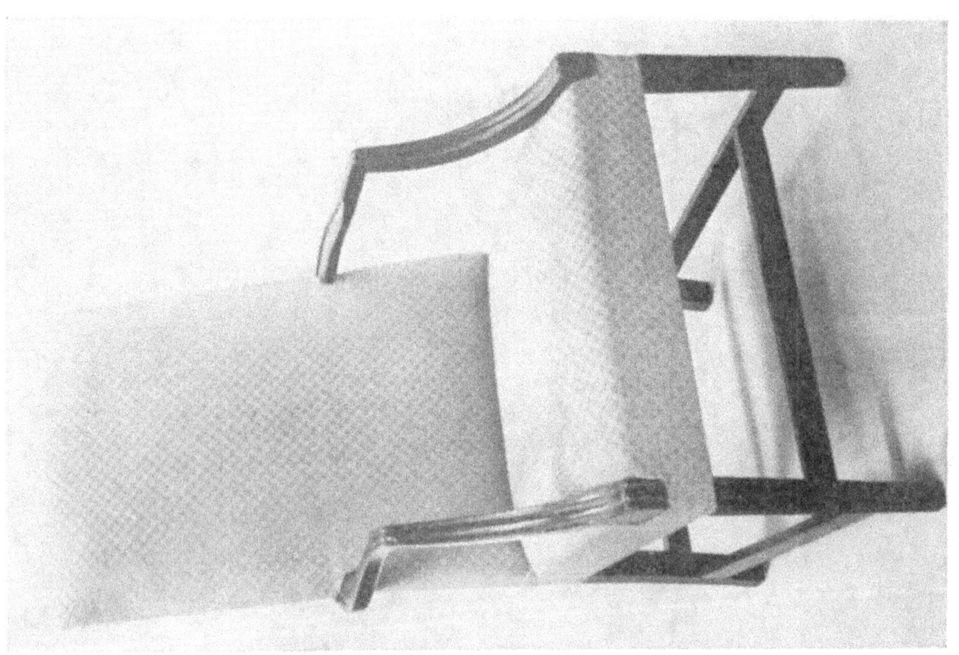

(LEFT) THE HEPPLEWHITE OVERLAPPING WITH THE SHERATON, *c. 1790–5*

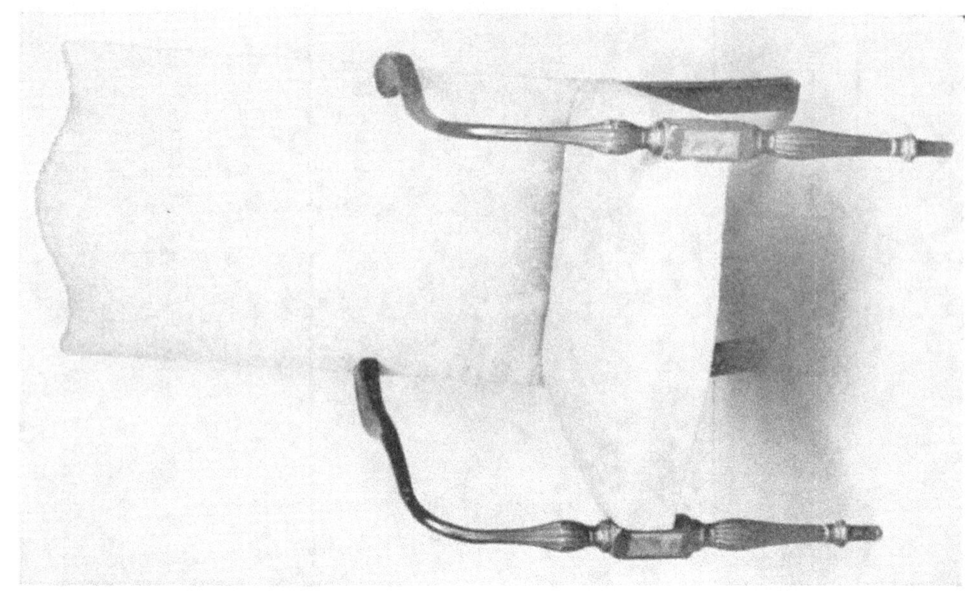

(RIGHT) THE NEW YORK SHERATON OF *c. 1800*

MAHOGANY OPEN-ARM BERGÈRE CHAIRS, AMERICAN

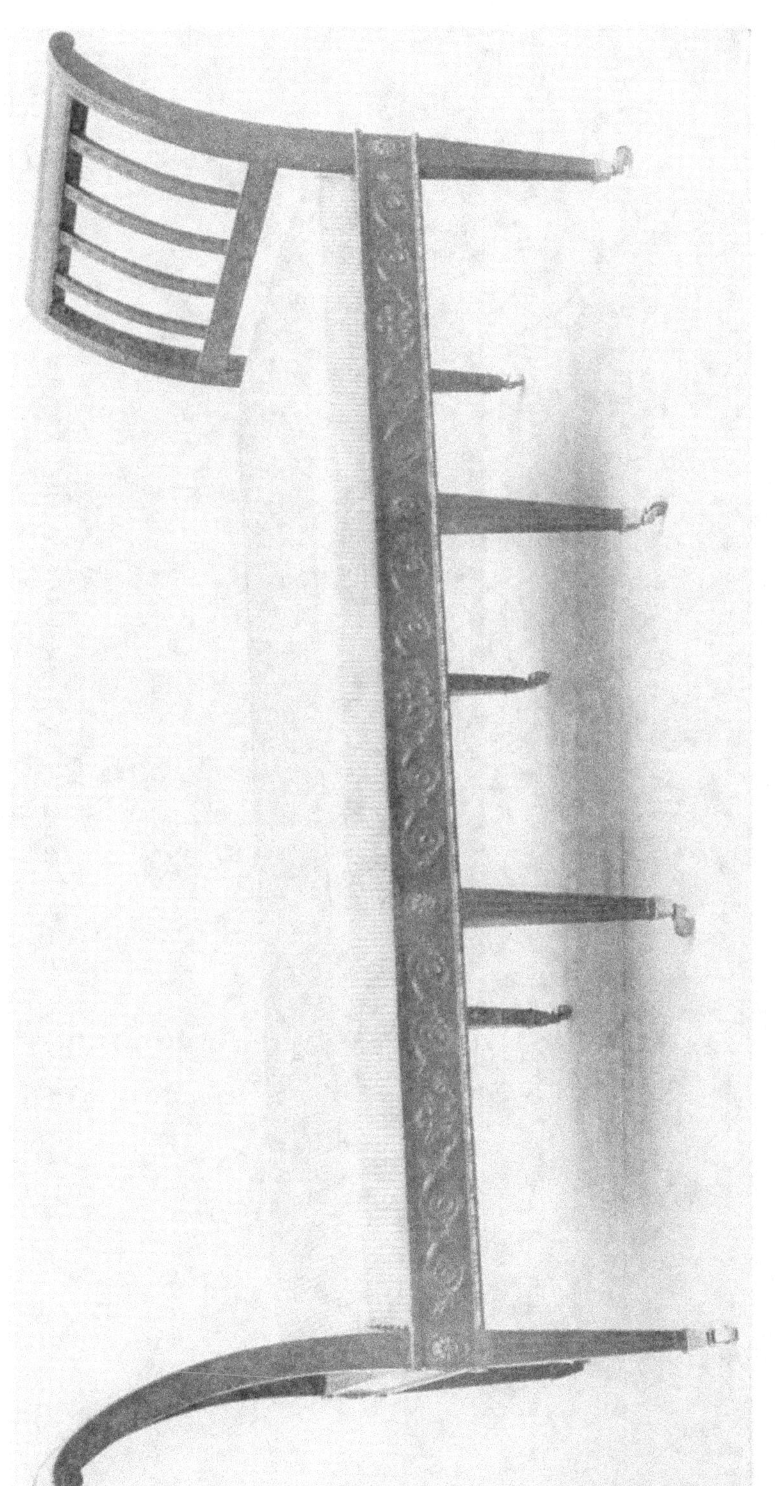

MAHOGANY SOFA BEDSTEAD, ENGLISH, *c. 1790.* THE SQUARE BACK OF THE SHERATON SCHOOL WITH TYPICAL ADAM CARVING, A "BRIDGE-PIECE"

SOFA BEDSTEAD TRANSITIONAL FROM SHERATON TO ADAM

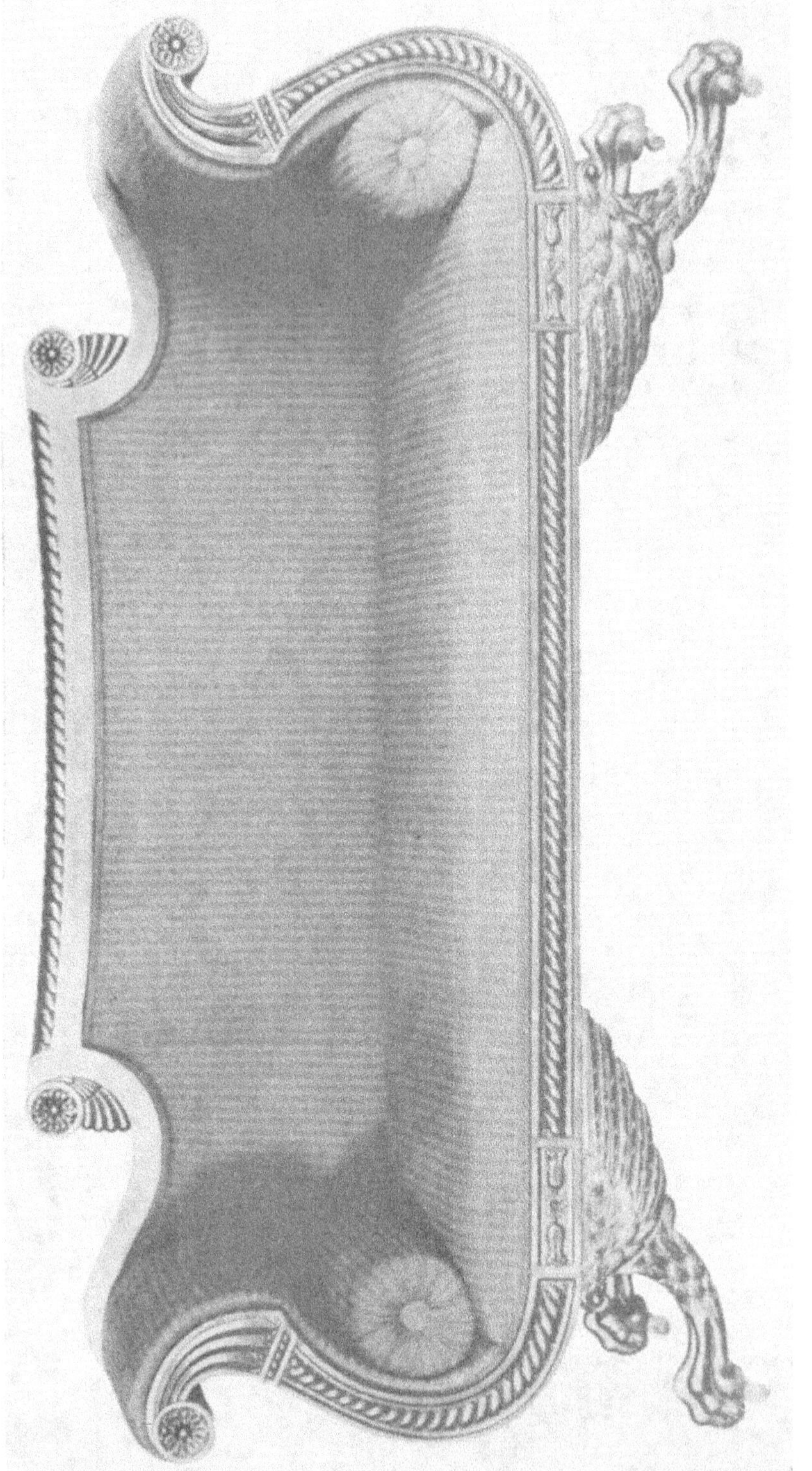

ENGLISH EMPIRE STYLE SETTEE; MAHOGANY INLAID WITH SATINWOOD, NEW YORK, *c. 1800*. THE CURVED TOP RAIL IS NOT AN ENGLISH DETAIL AT THIS PERIOD

ENGLISH EMPIRE STYLE SETTEE, *c.* 1800

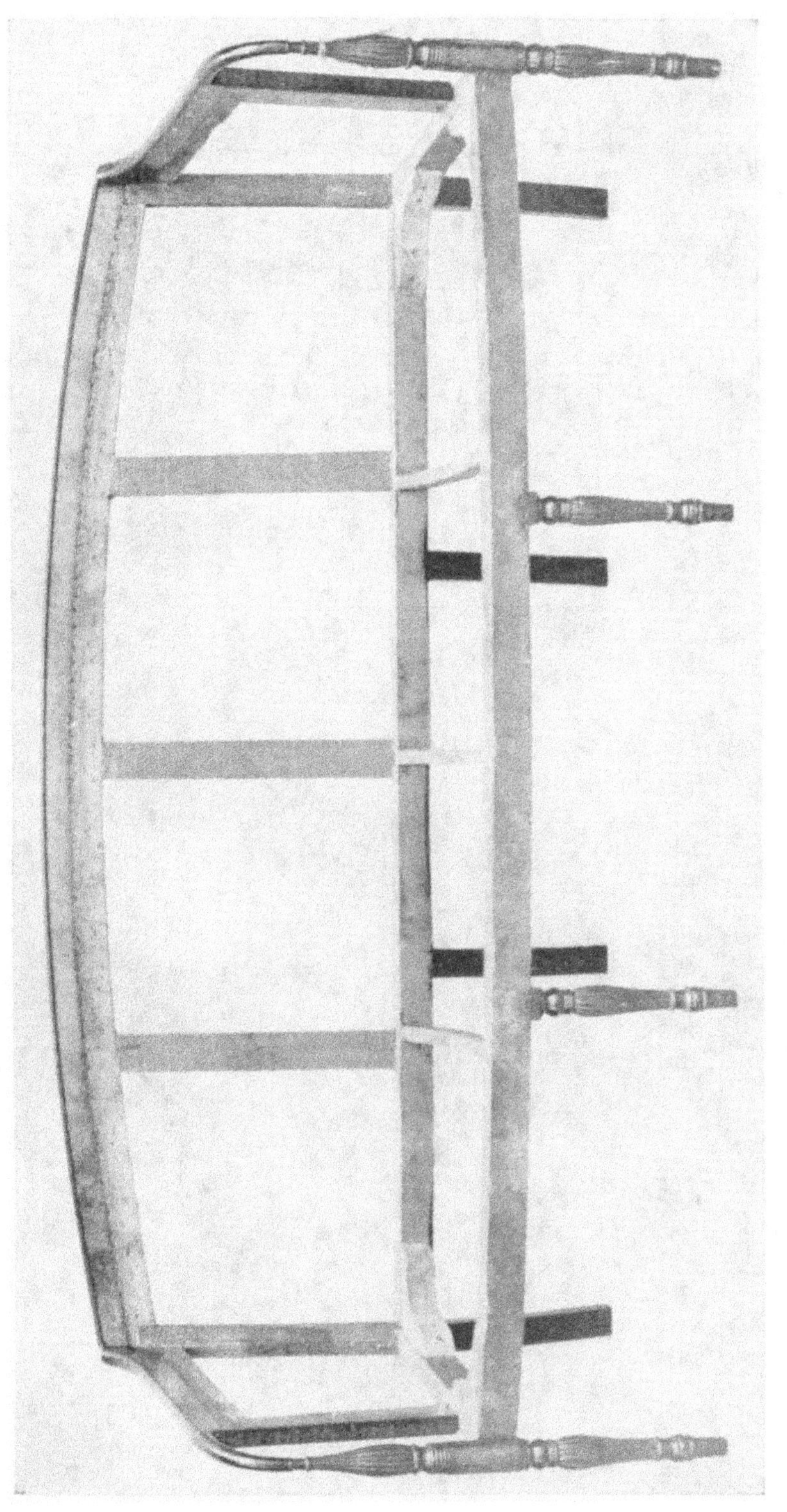

MAHOGANY SOFA. AMERICAN, EARLY *19*TH CENTURY

SOFA FRAME TRANSITIONAL FROM ENGLISH EMPIRE TO EARLY VICTORIAN

MAHOGANY DINING TABLE ON PEDESTAL SUPPORTS WITH FOUR COLUMNS AND SPLAY. CORNER FEET WITH CASTORS. ENGLISH EMPIRE STYLE, AMERICAN, *c. 1820–30*

MAHOGANY DINING TABLE ON CENTRAL PILLARS WITH FOUR SPLAY LEGS AND CASTORS. AMERICAN, STYLE OF DUNCAN PHYFE, *c. 1830*

ENGLISH EMPIRE AND DUNCAN PHYFE DINING TABLES

MAHOGANY CANTERBURY TABLE. EARLY *19*TH CENTURY, NEW YORK

MAHOGANY PEMBROKE TABLE. EARLY *19*TH CENTURY, NEW YORK

AMERICAN PEMBROKE AND CANTERBURY TABLES

MAHOGANY FLAP TABLE. AMERICAN, EARLY *19*TH CENTURY, DUNCAN PHYFE

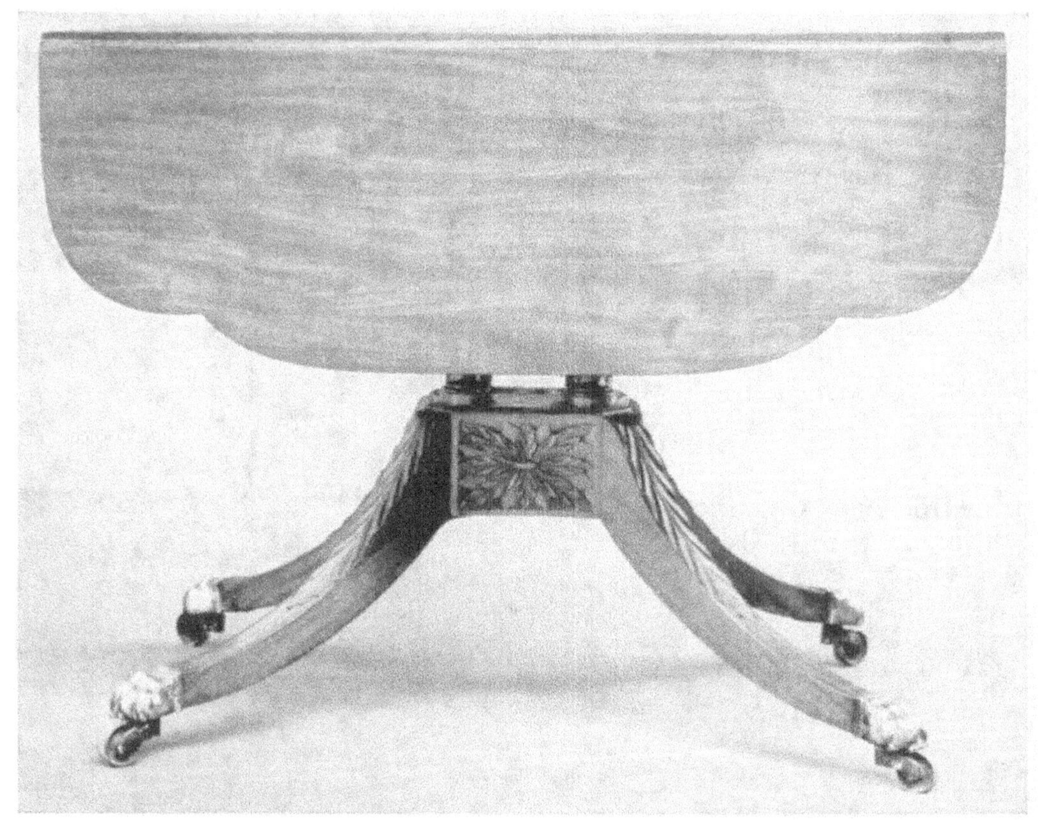

MAHOGANY FLAP TABLE. AMERICAN, EARLY *19*TH CENTURY, DUNCAN PHYFE

DUNCAN PHYFE FLAP TABLES

MAHOGANY SOFA TABLE. STYLE OF *1820*

MAHOGANY CENTER TABLE ON PILLARS AND WITH CLAWS. STYLE OF DUNCAN PHYFE, *c. 1830*

MAHOGANY CENTER AND SOFA TABLES

MAHOGANY HINGED-TOP CARD TABLE. LYRE STAND AND SPLAYED LEGS. STYLE OF DUNCAN PHYFE OF *c. 1830*

DUNCAN PHYFE HINGED-TOP CARD TABLE

GLOSSARY

ABACUS. The uppermost member of a column capital.

ACANTHUS. A leaf ornament based upon the foliage of the Acanthus spinosa, and used upon the capitals, friezes and cornices of the Corinthian and Composite orders of architecture.

ACORN TURNING. A term applied to turned ornaments resembling the acorn, and used chiefly on the backs of Jacobean chairs.

ANNULETS. Encircling bands of fillets upon the lower part of the Doric capital.

ANTHEMION. A Greek ornament based upon the foliage of the chamomile.

APRON. A strip next to or under the top of a table, chair or case piece, extending around or between the body, standard, legs or feet.

APRON PIECE. A term sometimes applied to wide curved rails in furniture.

ARCHIMEDEAN. Based upon the principles of the Archimedes screw.

ARCHITRAVE. The bottom member of an entablature; also a moulding surrounding a door or window opening.

ARMOIRE. An old press or wardrobe.

ARM SUPPORT. The upright supporting the front end of a chair arm. It may be either the fore leg extended or a separate member from the seatrail.

ARRIS. The sharp edge formed by two intersecting plain surfaces.

ASTRAGAL. A small convex beaded moulding.

BALUSTER. A small, slender turned member, usually with square base and cap.

BALUSTER TURNING. A turning characteristic of the Elizabethan and Jacobean periods.

BALUSTRADE. A row of balusters or turned pillars supporting a railing.

BANDING. A decorative inlay, strip or band of veneer which gives contrast, either in color or in grain, between itself and the surface decorated.

Banister. A corruption of the term "Baluster." The name is given also to the uprights in a chair back.

Baroque. An architectural style of Italian origin, characterized by conspicuous curves, broken scrolls and architectural decoration.

Barred Door. A framed-up door with tracerized patterns made up with mouldings and splats called bars. Introduced during the Chippendale and Sheraton periods.

Base. The bottom of an object, such as the bottom moulding of a column; also the plinth in carcase work.

Bead. A small rounded, convex moulding.

Bead and Butt. A term applied to the finish of flush panels in framing.

Bead and Flush. A bead worked and let in all around the panel.

Bead and Reel. An ornamental turning resembling beads and reels strung together alternately.

Bed Moulding. Any moulding placed under the crown or drip moulding of a cornice.

Bench End. The upright end of a church pew.

Bevel. A plain chamfer or cutting away of the edge in which two plain surfaces meet.

Bezel. The metal ring surrounding a clock-face glass; it is usually hinged.

Bidet. A small stand fitted for bedroom toilet use.

Bilsted. The wood of the sweet gum or liquidamber. Sometimes used in America in the latter eighteenth century in place of mahogany.

Bird's-Beak Lock. Used on piano falls, cylinder tables, and tambours; the bolt when thrust out resembles a bird's beak.

Block Foot. A square, vertical-sided foot at the base of a straight, untapered leg.

Block Front. Applied to case furniture in which drawer fronts and doors display swelling projections instead of panels.

Bodying in. A term in French polishing, meaning filling the grain of the wood.

Bolection. A rebated moulding fitting over the edges of parts of framing and raised above the surface.

Bombé. Outward swelling, curving or bulging. Applied to furniture with bulging contour.

Boss. An ornamented circular or oval protuberance at the intersection of mouldings.

BOTTLE TURNING. A detail of Dutch origin, so-called because of its resemblance to a bottle. Characteristic of the William and Mary period.

BOW TOP. A chair toprail with one low, unbroken curve across its whole width.

BRACKET CORNICE. A cornice moulding supported by brackets fixed to the frieze; a feature of Elizabethan and Jacobean furniture.

BREAK. The projection on a cornice, carcase or plinth when it stands forward or when the surface of the piece is broken.

BROKEN CORNER. A corner cut away from the convergent sides of a piece of furniture.

BUFFET. A sideboard or cupboard for the display of china or plate.

BULBOUS. Protuberant turnery of Dutch origin, and characteristic of turned work in the Queen Anne period.

BUN FOOT. A flattened glove or bun-shaped foot with slender ankle above.

BUREAU. A writing desk or chest of drawers or shelves for holding papers.

BURR. A growth or excrescence on the bole of a tree.

CABINET. Originally a small, private room for consultations but now applied to a form of cupboard enclosed by doors used for the display of china or plate.

CABINET HOOK. A small hook and eye applied to flaps and doors in cabinet and joinery work.

CABOCHON. A plain or round surface, convex or concave, enclosed within ornamentation.

CABRIOLE. A curved leg with an out-curving top or knee, an in-curving shaft or ankle and a shaped toe, resembling a conventionalized animal leg.

CAMBER. The convexity of a surface or arch.

CANDLE BOARD. A small ledge or shelf, characteristic of Sheraton work, fitting underneath a table top, for holding a candlestick.

CANOPY. A fixture over a throne or bedstead; also an ornamental Gothic projection over an arch, niche or doorway.

CANT. A chamfer, as in a canted or beveled edge.

CANTEEN. A case containing cutlery and table accessories.

CANTERBURY. A seat with a well to contain music, made especially for use at the piano; also a small table with drawer and shelves.

CAPITAL. The carved or moulded projecting member at the head of a pillar, shaft or column.

CARCASE. The body of a box-like piece of furniture, without ornament, doors or fittings.

CARTOUCHE. An ornamental form of unrolled scroll- or shield-shape, enclosing a plain surface often painted or inscribed.

CARIATIDE. A conventionalized female figure, supporting an arch or entablature.

CAVETTO. A round, concave moulding, generally described as a hollow.

CELLARET. A deep drawer or tray for bottles, in a sideboard.

CHAMFER. A bevelled cutting away of a corner or moulding.

CHASING. A decorative, incised finish applied to metal mounts.

CHEQUER. Decoration in squares differently shaded or colored alternately, as in a checker-board.

CHESTERFIELD. An overstuffed couch with double ends.

CHEVAL GLASS. A large glass or mirror swinging between framed-up supports.

CINQUEFOIL. Gothic foliation having five cusps or foils.

CLASH. The figure in oak; also called felt and silver grain.

CLAW AND BALL. A carved detail of ancient origin resembling a bird's claw clasped around a ball.

CLUB FOOT. A foot used usually in conjunction with a straight type of cabriole leg, in early Queen Anne and Chippendale work.

CLUSTERED COLUMNS. A Chippendale Gothic detail, consisting of columns placed together in clusters.

COCKED BEADING. A rounded moulding projecting beyond an edge or surface; when sunk below the surface it is a sunk bead; when separated by a narrow sunk fillet or bead it is a quirked bead.

COLLARED TOE. The base of a table or chair leg with an ornamental band.

COLONIAL GEORGIAN. A style of furniture and decoration based upon the work of eighteenth century, British settlers in the United States.

COMMODE. A small cabinet or pedestal for bedroom use; a chest of drawers.

COMPO. An abbreviation of the term "composition," a substitute for wood carving; also called "stucco." Its chief constituents are whiting, glue and resin.

CONCAVE. A hollow, curved line or surface.

CONFIDANTE. A sofa with seats at each end.

CONSOLE. A projecting bracket, usually of scroll-form, applied indiscriminately in furniture to console or bracket tables and to brackets under beams.

CONTOUR. The profile of a moulding or of an object.

CONVOLUTE. Rolled in the form of a scroll.

CORINTHIAN. An ornate order of Grecian architecture which possesses a bell-shaped capital adorned with conventionalized acanthus leaves rising out of caulicoli or cabbage-like forms.

CORNICE. The crowning member, as of a capital or column; the top member of an entablature; the projecting mouldings between the walls and ceiling of a room.

CORONA. A flat projecting member in a cornice between the cymatium or cap moulding and the bed moulding below.

COURT CUPBOARD. An Elizabethan form of cabinet; a chest on legs with a recessed cupboard above.

COVE. A large hollow moulding or recess applied to furniture, generally acting as a cornice; also synonymous with niche, a curved recess which often contains a statuette or a vase-like ornament.

CREDENCE. A Gothic name for a side- or re-table.

CRESTING. An ornamental topping, usually of a chair, settee or case piece.

CROSSRAIL. The horizontal bar or splat in a chair back.

CUPID'S BOW. A variety of compound or serpentine curve much used in the toprails of Chippendale chairs.

CURL. A natural figure in wood, resembling a feather; it is obtained by cutting at the intersection of a large bough with the tree trunk.

CUSP. A Gothic ornamental detail, consisting of a point or knob frequently carved, projecting from the intersection of two curves.

CYLINDER. The fall of a writing table in the shape of a quadrant or arc of a circle.

CYMA CURVE. A wave curve, of double or compound curvature.

CYMA RECTA. A classic moulding obtained from a horizontal wave, called also an ogee.

CYMA REVERSA. A classic moulding obtained from a vertical wave, called also a reversed ogee.

Dentils. Rectangular, equally-spaced blocks, usually placed in a cornice and probably an ornamental survival of the structural projecting ends of horizontal roof timbers.

Diaperwork. Surface decoration consisting of a design in regular repeats that seem to form diagonal patterns.

Dished Corner. A table corner slightly hollowed out to hold a candlestick.

Dog Ear. A projecting rectangular ornament at the head of a door frame or paneling. Much used in early Georgian work.

Dog-tooth. An ornamental detail characteristic of Early English work, consisting of a small pyramidal repeat ornament used chiefly in mouldings.

Dolphin Hinge. So called because of its resemblance to the contour of a dolphin; used in conjunction with quadrant stays in secretaries.

Doric. A massive order of Grecian architecture ascribed to the Dorians.

Dovetail. A joint so named because of its resemblance to the tail of a dove.

Dowel. A wooden pin fastening together two pieces of chair or cabinet-work.

Drawer Slip. The grooved slip or strip that holds a drawer bottom.

Drop Ornament. A turned ornament used in Jacobean work; also a decorative detail resembling a husk in eighteenth century decoration.

Dropped Seat. A seat made concave so that its middle and front are lower than its sides.

Dumb Waiter. A type of dinner wagon.

Dust Board. A horizontal division between drawers, introduced to prevent tampering with their contents and as a preventive against dust; also called a dust bottom.

Ebonize. To impart to wood, by means of staining and polishing, a finish resembling ebony.

Echinus. A Grecian moulding with carved eggs and darts as a decorative feature; also called necking.

Edging. A small, solid, protecting strip let in on the edge of a veneered surface.

Egg and Tongue Moulding. Also called egg and dart. Used largely with architectural mouldings of a classical character; also used in Georgian furniture and decoration.

ELIZABETHAN. Relating to the Renaissance style of architecture and woodwork in England, prevailing during the reign of Queen Elizabeth.

ENAMEL. A finish for furniture prepared by coating the wood with whiting and size, rubbing down level and then finishing off with a transparent French polish; also a fusible, glass-like substance, nearly opaque, used in decorating furniture mounts.

ENDIVE SCROLL. A carved ornament belonging to the Chippendale period and derived from the endive leaf.

ENGRAVING. A term applied to the decoration of marquetry, by which a relief effect is produced by engraving fine lines on the veneers, the lines being afterwards rubbed in with a colored composition to render them visible.

ENTABLATURE. An architectural term applied to the members above the column, composed of architrave, frieze and cornice; in furniture the term is sometimes synonymous with cornice.

ENTASIS. The swell or slightly convex curve in a round or angular pillar, to correct the hollow effect caused by an optical illusion.

ESCRITOIRE. A writing desk or bureau.

ESCUTCHEON. A shield charged with armorial bearings or other devices; also a brass fitting for a keyhole.

EVOLUTE. A recurrent wave motif for frieze or band decoration.

EXTRADOS. The outside curved line or surface of an arch.

FACING. Applied to furniture construction, a thinner covering of wood upon a thicker groundwork.

FALDSTOOL. A portable, folding seat similar to a camp stool.

FALL. The falling front of a bureau, *secrétaire,* writing desk or piano.

FASCIA. A broad fillet or plain band.

FAUN. A legendary demi-god, represented as half goat and half man; used decoratively in work of the Adam period.

FEATHER-EDGING. A feather pattern of veneer or marquetry banding.

FESTOON. A carved, painted or inlaid decoration in the form of a wreath or garland.

FIDDLE BACK. A figured veneer resembling the finely marked sycamore used in violin backs.

FILIGREE. Ornamental work in gold or silver wire.

FILLET. A small slip or ledge used for supporting shelves; also a small band or fascia.

FINIAL. A decorative crowning device at the corners or middle or any projecting upright.

FISH SKIN. The skin of fish dressed and dyed. Used for covering clock cases, and especially suitable in combination with silver mounts and fittings.

FITMENT. Any article made and fixed to a wall or room, including paneling, chimney-pieces and fitted furniture.

FIELDED. Applied to a panel moulded, sunk, or raised, or broken up into smaller panels.

FLEMISH SCROLL. A Baroque scroll with the curve broken by an angle.

FLUSH. Level or even with an adjoining surface.

FLUTING. A series of hollow, rounded furrows or channels around a pillar, shaft, leg or frieze.

FLY RAIL. The side rail of a flap table, which opens to support the flap.

FOIL. The point formed by the intersection of two circular arcs; a Gothic decorative detail used in the trefoil, quatrefoil.

FOLIATED. Pertaining to the use of foils.

FRET. Interlaced, ornamental work, sometimes applied on a solid background, sometimes perforated; used in the Chinese Chippendale style; also called fretwork and fretting.

FRIEZE. That plain or ornamental member of an entablature which lies between the cornice or crown and the architrave or lintel.

GADROON. A carved and curved, fluted or ruffled ornament for edges; characteristic of Elizabethan and Jacobean woodwork.

GALLERY. A raised rim of fretwork or metal bars surrounding a table top or at the back of a sideboard top.

GEORGIAN. Pertaining to work executed during the reigns of the first three Georges from 1714 to 1820.

GIRANDOLE. A branched candle-holder or wall candle-bracket used in eighteenth century interior decoration, often attached to a mirror.

GOTHIC. The architecture and woodwork of the Middle Ages, the 14th, 15th and 16th centuries.

Gros Point. A kind of coarse-stitch embroidery used chiefly for upholstering seating furniture and covering screens.

Grotesque. Monstrous or comic figures or heads used as ornaments.

Gueridon. A small, round stand, usually for candles.

Guilloche. A running ornament composed of curved, interlacing lines.

Hanging Stile. The frame member of a door upon which the hinges or pivots are fixed.

Harlequin. An automatic table invented by Sheraton, in which the center part rises when its flaps are raised.

Head. The upper member or rail of a door, also the top member of a framework.

Herring Boning. A veneered detail of Queen Anne work, consisting of narrow bands of striped veneer cut obliquely and placed together, resembling a herring-bone pattern.

Hood. A shaped top, as in a curio cabinet, clock or bureau.

Hoop Back. A chair-back in which uprights and toprail continue in an unbroken line of curves.

Housing. The process of recessing or grooving one piece of wood into another.

Husk. A form of drop or pendent ornament taken from nature, used in 18th century woodwork.

Hutch. A chest on legs, with wood doors.

Impost. The pillar from which an arch springs and on which it rests.

Incised Ornament. Ornament cut in or engraved; sixteenth century cabinetwork was sometimes so ornamented, the incisions being afterwards filled in with a colored composition.

Inlaying. A decorative process in which geometrical or naturalistic patterns, bands or other ornamental devices are grooved or cut into a groundwork.

Intarsia. Inlaid, decorative work in which the design is cut and fitted into corresponding cavities in a veneered or solid ground.

In the White. Cabinetwork in the natural wood, before it is filled, stained or polished.

Intrados. The under or inside curved line or surface of an arch.

Ionic. A graceful order of Grecian architecture, distinguished by the ish-ioned scrolls or volutes of its column capital.

Jacobean. The style of architecture and woodwork of the James I p od, immediately following the Elizabethan.

Japanning. Originally synonymous with lacquering, the term now de otes a coating with paint, preparatory to decorating.

Jardiniere. A box or pedestal specially designed to hold flowers.

Joint Stool. A joined or joinery stool.

Joyner. The mediæval craftsman in wood, before the distinction was ade between the cabinetmaker, who made furniture, and the joiner, who ade fixed or architectural woodwork.

Kettle Front. A swelling or bulging front of earlier date and sh per curves than a bombé front.

Keystone. A wedge-shaped member inserted at the crown of an arch, erv-ing to bind it together, either structurally or in a decorative sense.

Kidney Table. A table in shape resembling a kidney; introduced by S era-ton in pedestal writing tables.

Knee. The upper, convex curve of a cabriole leg.

Ladder Back. Applied to a chair back with slats or horizontal rails r em-bling the rungs of a ladder.

Laminate. To build up in layers.

Landscape Panel. A panel placed with the grain of the wood ru ning horizontally.

Lattice. Resembling a network, as in lattice-back Sheraton chairs or rass lattice work in bookcase doors.

Lectern. An ecclesiastical reading-desk.

Linen-fold Panel. A panel bearing a Tudor ornament in which fo s of linen are conventionalized.

Listel. An alternative term for fillet, a flat, plain moulding.

Livery Cupboard. A cupboard in which bread was kept for distril tion to the poor.

Locking Stile. The stile of a door carrying the lock; in double doors lled a meeting stile.

Loose Seat. A stuffed removable seat frame let into the framing of a chair.

LOO TABLE. An oval table made for the game of loo.

LOPER. The sliders supporting a bureau fall, and also the sliders of an extending dining-table.

LOTUS. An Egyptian ornamental form derived from the flower of the lotus lily.

LOW RELIEF. A term applied to carving or built-up decoration in which the ornamental surface does not project far from the groundwork.

LOZENGE. Diamond-shaped, an ornamental feature of Elizabethan and Adam overlays.

LUNETTE. A crescent or semi-circular, plain or decorated surface or window opening.

MARQUETRY. Inlaid, decorative work in which several thicknesses of veneer are cut and built up into a sheet before being glued to the core or groundwork; also spelled "marqueterie."

MASQUE. A full face (human, animal or grotesque) used without the rest of the body, as a form of ornament.

MEDALLION. A plaque or medal, with figures or heads in low relief.

MITRE. The joint in a moulding formed in changing its direction.

MODILLIONS. Enriched brackets or large moulded dentils under a cornice of an entablature on furniture or a room.

MODULE. A unit of measure in design by which proportions are decided.

MORTISE. A hole cut into a structural member to receive a projection upon another member called a tenon.

MOSAIC. Decoration composed of small pieces decoratively arranged as to form or color.

MOTHER-OF-PEARL. The hard and brilliantly colored internal layer of shells.

MOTTLED. A speckled or variegated grain in veneer, giving a spotty effect.

MOULDING. A shaped projection of linear form used to break the continuity of surfaces for decorative effect.

MOUNT. A piece of decorative hardware or metal ornament on a piece of furniture.

MUNTING, MUNTIN OR MULLION. Horizontal or vertical division bars in doors, windows or framing of furniture or architecture.

NECKING. Any small band or moulding near the top of a shaft, pillar, impost or column.

NICHE. A depression or recess in a wall or piece of cabinetwork, to receive a bust, statuette or other plastic ornament.

NULLING. Turned or carved ornament, quadrant-shaped in section, used on friezes and mouldings in Jacobean work.

OGEE. A form made by two opposite cyma or wave curves with their convex sides meeting in a point.

ORMOLU. A composition of brass and zinc that resembles gold, used for casting furniture mounts.

OTTOMAN. A seat without a back, of Turkish origin.

OVAL. Egg-shaped; incorrectly applied to an ellipse.

OVERSTUFFED. Applied to seating furniture in which the upholstering completely hides the wooden frame.

OVOLO. A rounded, convex moulding.

OXIDIZING. A finish imparted to metalwork by chemical treatment.

OYSTERING. Veneer showing cross-sectional grain in irregular concentric rings, resembling the markings on oyster shells.

PARCHMENT PANEL. Another name for a linen-fold panel.

PATERA. A small, circular or elliptical, carved ornament applied to friezes, pediments, chair legs.

PATINA. The surface color or finish on wood, metal or stone resulting from wear or polishing.

PEDESTAL. A stand for statues or statuettes; also a moulded base supporting a cupboard, chest of drawers, sideboard or table.

PEDIMENT. An architectural gable or cresting for cabinetwork, triangular, segmental or scrolled.

PEMBROKE TABLE. A table with a fixed frame and flaps on each side, supported on brackets.

PENDANT. A hanging ornament.

PERPENDICULAR STYLE. The final stage of the Gothic style in England, belonging to the late fifteenth and early sixteenth centuries.

PETIT POINT. A fine-stitch embroidery used chiefly for upholstering seating furniture and screens.

PIE-CRUST TABLE. A small circular table with the edge curved and raised above the surface of its top.

Pier Glass. A wall mirror hanging between windows, usually above a semicircular or pier table.

Pigeonholes. Divisions or compartments in a stationery case, bureau or escritoire.

Pilaster. A slightly projecting pillar, generally with moulded or ornamented base and cap.

Pillar. Synonymous with column or shaft.

Pillar and Claw. Applied to circular tables of the 18th and early 19th centuries, made with a center pillar and claw feet.

Planted. Applied to mouldings that are mitred and affixed to furniture separately from the framing or groundwork.

Plaque. A circular or elliptical medallion of porcelain, Sèvres, or Wedgwood, used as furniture decoration.

Plinth. The framed-up base or bottom part or carcase work or of a pillar, shaft or column.

Pollard. A peculiar growth at the top of a tree, yielding valuable figured veneers; it is caused by lopping off the top boughs.

Pounce. A colored powder used by marqueterie cutters to copy and mark out designs.

Press. A dwarf cupboard or wardrobe used for storing linen.

Profile. The outline or contour of an object or a moulding; also a side view.

Projection. Applied to the overhang of a cornice or moulding.

Quartered. Cutting a log into four quarters through its center and then in parallel cuts into boards.

Quatrefoil. A Gothic form suggesting the conventional adaptation of a four-leafed clover; it is formed by four intersecting curves enclosed within a circle.

Quirk. The narrow groove or sunk fillet at the side of a bead.

Rail. A horizontal member in the frame of cabinetwork or paneling.

Rake. The angle or slant as of a chair-back.

Recessed Stretcher. Front stretcher set back between the two side stretchers, as in some tables, chairs and case pieces.

Reeding. Semi-circular, moulded projections similar to inverted flutes on turned shafts and pillars.

Renaissance. Re-birth; a style of architecture originating in Italy in the fourteenth century and marking the advent of modern times.

Ribband Back. A back with ribbon motif ornament, found in Chippendale work.

Ribband Decoration. Carved or inlaid ornament resembling ribbon; found in eighteenth century furniture.

Rim. An edge or projection around tray or table top, also underneath the tops of shaped tables.

Rising Stretcher. A stretcher rising in a curve between the legs it braces.

Rococo. A style of architecture and ornamentation belonging to the 18th century, displaying ornate curves, rocks, shells and other conventionalized, rustic forms.

Roe. Pertaining to figured veneer showing a spotty arrangement as of fish roe.

Romayne Work. Ornamentation using human heads upon roundels or medallions.

Rosette. A round or foliated ornament or disc.

Rotten Stone. A soft, powdered stone used with oil in polishing.

Roundel. A circular background for ornamentation.

Salient Angle. An outside or projecting angle or advancing corner.

Saltire. An arrangement of stretchers in X-form.

Scallop. A carved ornament resembling an escalloped shell.

Scotia. A hollow or concave moulding, found in the bases of columns of the Ionic, Corinthian and Composite orders of architecture.

Scroll. An ornament of convolute form.

Scrutoire. An enclosed writing cabinet or table; also called escritoire.

Seat Rail. The frame of a chair, bench or settee on which the seat is built.

Secretary. A case piece with falling front used for writing purposes; usually applied to the deep drawer with hinged front.

Serpentine. A term applied to a piece of furniture in which the front lines are wavy or curved.

Settee. A light seat with low back and arms, sometimes upholstered.

Settle. An old form of wooden seat with ends and a back.

Shaded Marquetry. A process of shading marquetry, effected with hot sand.

Show Wood. The wood parts of an upholstered seating piece that are seen.

Sideboard Table. A side or serving table, the progenitor of the eighteenth century sideboard.

Skiver. A thin layer of leather used for lining table tops and obtained from the split hide.

Slats. Horizontal rails in a chair-back; also the cross-pieces supporting a bed spring or mattress.

Sliders. Flaps or shelves which pull or slide out of a carcase.

Socle. A plain block acting as a plinth, pedestal or base to a case piece.

Sofa Table. A table with flaps at the ends, first designed by Sheraton.

Soffit. The underside of a projecting decorative member or moulding in a piece of furniture.

Spade Foot. A four-sided foot at the bottom of a tapered leg, its outline resembling a spade.

Spandrel. The triangular surface bounded by the outer curves of two archs and the horizontal line above them. Where there is but one arch the vertical line from the spring of the arch forms the third side of the triangle.

Spindle. A small turned pillar used in or applied to furniture.

Spinet. An early form of stringed instrument, one of the forerunners of the pianoforte.

Spiral Turning. Twisted, turned work characteristice of chair and table legs of the seventeenth century.

Splat. The central, vertical member of a chair-back.

Spoon Back. A term applied to Queen Anne chair backs, which from the side resemble the curve in a spoon and fit the contour of the body.

Squab. A loose cushion-seat for a chair or couch.

Stall. A seat for an ecclesiastical dignitary or choir member in a church.

Standard. The upright supports of a toilet-glass frame or the supporting frame of a table or case piece.

Stile. The vertical member in the frame of a piece of cabinetwork or paneling, also the outside vertical members of a door.

Strapwork. Carved ornament derived from bands frequently interlacing, used especially in the Elizabethan and Jacobean periods.

STRETCHER. A brace between the legs of a chair, table or case piece.

STUCCO. A fine plaster-like substance used for modeled decorations, chiefly during the Adam period.

STUD. A small metal piece with projecting head, used for supporting adjustable shelves; also a decorative nail-head.

SUNK PANEL. A sinkage in a pilaster, pillar or column.

SURBASE. A moulded member above the real base or plinth in architecture or furniture.

SWAG. A form of swinging or suspended ornament, usually drapery or festoons of flowers and fruits.

SWAN-NECK. A curved pediment found on Chippendale cabinets.

SWELL FRONT. A convexly curved front of a case piece.

SWIVEL HOOK. A reversible, pivoted hook sometimes applied in wardrobes.

TALL-BOY. A double chest of drawers consisting of one carcase above another.

TAMBOUR. A flexible shutter or desk-fall, made by gluing thin strips of wood to a linen backing.

TAPER. A diminishing form characteristic of eighteenth century furniture legs.

TENON. A projection cut at the end of one piece of wood to fit into the corresponding hole or mortise in the piece to which it is to be fastened.

TERMINAL FIGURE. A conventionalized human bust on a pedestal.

TERN FEET. Feet consisting of a three-scroll arrangement found in Chippendale work.

TESTER. The upper part or canopy of a high-post bedstead.

TOPRAIL. The top member of a chairback, settee or bench.

TORUS. A bold convex, cushion-like moulding of semi-circular or rounded profile.

TRACERY. Ornamental penetrations or overlays in Gothic work; synonymous with fretwork in Chippendale work; pierced metal lattice work in Sheraton doors.

TREFOIL. An architectural feature characteristic of the Gothic style and consisting of three arcs, formed by their intersection and inscribed in a circle.

TRESTLE TABLE. The oldest form of table known, consisting of boards placed upon trestles.

TURKEYWORK. A form of embroidery popular in the seventeenth century.

TRIPTYCH. An altar piece made of three folding or hinged members—a center and two side compartments; also applied to mirror frames.

TUDOR ROSE. A conventionalized, carved rose characteristic of early Tudor furniture and woodwork.

URN. A vase-shaped vessel or ornament characteristic of the Adam period.

VENEER. A layer or layers of figured wood glued together crosswise, upon solid or built-up wood.

VOLUTE. A spiral scroll used in Ionic, Corinthian, and Composite capitals.

WAINSCOT. Boards used for panelwork as in wainscot chairs. Low panelwork itself.

WATER GILDING. Covering ormolu mounts with a thin deposit of gold and mercury.

WATER LEAF. An ornamental detail resembling an elongated laurel leaf; used chiefly on Hepplewhite and Sheraton furniture.

WAX INLAYING. A species of incised work filled in with colored wax.

WHAT-NOT. A tier of shelves supported by turned posts.

YORKSHIRE DRESSER. A dresser with a low back made in oak or deal and peculiar to Yorkshire.

CHRONOLOGICAL TABLE OF THE SOVEREIGNS OF FRANCE AND ENGLAND FROM THE 15th TO THE EARLY 19th CENTURIES

ENGLAND

House of Tudor

Henry VII. 1485-1509
Henry VIII. 1509-1547
Edward VI. 1547-1553
Mary. 1553-1558
Elizabeth. 1558-1603

House of Stuart

James I. 1603-1625
Charles I. 1625-1649
Protectorate of Cromwell. 1649-1660

Restoration of Monarchy

Charles II. 1660-1685
James II. 1685-1689

House of Orange

William III (and Mary). 1689-1703
Anne (of Denmark). 1703-1714

House of Brunswick

George I. 1714-1727
George II. 1727-1760
George III. 1760-1820
George IV. 1820-1830

FRANCE

Louis XII. 1498-1515

Francis I. 1515-1547

Henry II. 1547-1559

Francis II. (The Imbecile) 1559-1560

Charles IX. 1560-1574

Henry III. 1574-1589

Henry IV. 1589-1610

Louis XIII. 1610-1643

Louis XIV. 1643-1715

The Regency. 1715-1723

Louis XV. 1715-1774

Louis XVI. 1774-1793

The Revolution. 1791

The Directory. 1795-1799

Napoleon—Emperor. 1799-1815

Note. The Calendar in England was changed in 1702, therefore the dates of 1702 or 1703 for the accession of Anne are both correct, according to which of the two Calendars is implied.

NOTABLE EVENTS AND DATES IN AMERICAN HISTORY

1580–1600 Attempts of Raleigh to found colony in Virginia.

1607 Founding of Jamestown Colony. Province of Virginia.

1609 Henry Hudson sails up the Hudson River.

1615 Fort Nassau (now Albany) founded.

1620 Landing of the Pilgrim Fathers in Massachusetts.

1626 New Amsterdam (New York) founded.

1630 Massachusetts Colony founded.

1639 Royal Charter of Maine granted.

1662 Connecticut Colony founded.

1663 Rhode Island Colony founded.

1681–2 Philadelphia laid out by William Penn.

1690–1760 Struggles with the French.

1702 French colonize Mobile.

1718 French colonize New Orleans

1733 The Molasses Act.

1763 Treaty of Paris; England acquires Florida and Louisiana.

1765 Stamp Act.

1770 Tea Tax (Townshend Revenue Act).

1775 Battles of Bunker Hill, Lexington and Concord.

1776 Declaration of Independence.

1778 Alliance with France. Lafayette and Talleyrand.

1781 Surrender of Cornwallis.

1789 Constitution of the United States. Inauguration of Washington.

1812 War with England.

CRAFTSMEN AND AUTHORS OF DESIGN BOOKS IN ENGLAND IN THE EIGHTEENTH CENTURY

Adam, Robert and James, Works in Architecture. Various dates. Four Volumes.

Brunetti, G., "Ornaments." 1st Edition 1731, 2nd Edition 1736.

Chippendale, Thomas, "Gentleman and Cabinetmaker's Director." 1st Edition 1754, 2nd Edition 1755, 3rd Edition 1762.

Thomas Chippendale was born at Otley, in Yorkshire, in 1718, the son of John Chippendale, a joiner. He married Catherine Redshaw in London in 1748, and Elizabeth Davis in 1776. He died in 1779 and was buried in St. Martins-in-the-Fields, London. He had, as first partner, James Rannie, and afterwards Thomas Haig. The authenticated work of Chippendale, at Nostell Priory, Wakefield, Harewood House in Yorkshire and elsewhere is all billed as "Dr to Chippendale, Haig & Co." He left children, including one Thomas Chippendale, Jr.

Chippendale, Jr., Thomas, "Ornaments." 1779.

Cipriani, Giovanni Battista, "Ornaments." 1786.

Columbani, Placido, "Ornaments." 1775. "Capitals, Etc." 1776.

Copeland, H., "New Book of Ornaments." 1746.

Crunden, J., "Cabinetmaker's Darling." 1765.

Darly, Matthias, "Sixty Vases." 1767. (See also Edwards & Darly.)

Edwards & Darly, "Chinese Designs." 1754.

Gibbs, James, "Shields and Tablets." 1731.

Hepplewhite & Co., A., "Cabinetmaker and Upholsterer's Guide." 1st Edition 1788, 2nd Edition 1789, 3rd Edition 1794. (See also Shearer, etc. London Book of Prices. 1788.)

George Hepplewhite of Cripplegate in the City of London must have been a cabinetmaker of some renown, and there is some evidence to show that his style influenced, in furniture, that of Robert Adam. (*q.v.*) He died in 1786, and his book was published by his widow,

Alice, under the name of "A. Hepplewhite & Co." Of his working life nothing is known.

Ince & Mayhew (William Ince & Thomas Mayhew), "System of Household Furniture." 1763.

The style of this book so closely resembles the "Director" of Chippendale that there is a strong presumption that the same designers were engaged on both, and that neither of the two was the actual work either of Ince & Mayhew or of Chippendale.

Johnson, Thomas, "Designs for Picture Frames." 1758. "New Designs." 1761.

Langley, Thomas & Batty, "Builder's Treasury of Designs." 1745.

Batty Langley attempted to revive the Gothic style in England, an endeavor which called forth the derision of Horace Walpole. Chippendale definitely adopted a debased form of the Gothic for some of the designs in the "Director."

Lock & Copeland, "Ornaments." 1st Edition 1752, 2nd Edition 1758. (See Matthias Lock.)

Lock, Matthias, "Six Tables." 1746.
"Book of Tables, etc." 1768.
"Six Sconces." 1768.
"Pier Frames, etc." 1769.
"New Book of Foliage." 1769.

Manwaring, Robert, "Carpenter's Compleat Guide." 1765.
"Cabinet and Chair Maker's Best Friend." 1765.
"Chair Maker's Guide." 1766.

Milton, Columbani, Crunden & Overton, "Chimney-Piece Maker's Assistant." 1766.

Paine, William, "Builder's Companion." 1st Edition 1761, 2nd Edition 1765, 3rd Edition 1769.
"Practical Builder." 1st Edition 1774, 2nd Edition 1793.
"Carpenter's Repository." 1778.

Pastorini, B., "Designs for Girandoles." 1775.

Pergolesi, Michel Angelo, "Designs." 1777.

Pergolesi was one of the artists employed in painted decoration for furniture, ceilings and walls by the brothers, Robert and James Adam, in company with Antonio Zucchi, Angelica Kauffmann and Cipriani.

Richardson, George, "Ceilings." 1st Edition 1776, 2nd Edition 1793.
"Chimney-pieces." 1781.
"Designs for Tripods, Etc." 1793.

Shearer, Hepplewhite and others. "The Cabinetmaker's London Book of Prices." 1788. (Several editions followed.)

This is a wonderful production, in which every operation in the trade is described and priced. It was used up to 1870 as the standard book in the piecework shops, where jobs were given out without estimating and priced up by the maker in minute detail. It was possible, with one well acquainted with the Price Book, to make his work come out at a higher price as compared with another not so well informed, hence the term "Knowing his book" which arose at this time.

Shearer, Thomas, "Designs for Household Furniture." 1788. (See Sheraton.)

There is no doubt that Shearer was largely the originator of what we know as the Sheraton style, a credit which he shares with Hepplewhite. Note the date of his book and compare with that of Sheraton.

Sheraton, Thomas, "Cabinetmaker and Upholsterer's Drawing Book." 1st Edition 1791, 2nd Edition (2 vols.) 1793, 3rd Edition 1802. "Cabinet Dictionary." 1803.

"Cabinetmaker, Upholsterer & General Artist's Encyclopædia." 1804. (Projected in 125 folio parts. Part 1 only, completed.)

Thomas Sheraton was born at Stockton-on-Tees, County Durham, in 1750, and died in London in 1806.

Stalker & Parker, "A Treatise on Japanning, Etc." (Lacquering) 1688.

Swan, Abraham, "Designs in Carpentry." 1759.

Tijou, J., "Designs for Ironwork." 1693.

(Tijou made the fine iron gates of Hampton Court Palace on the river front.)

Wallis, N., "Book of Ornaments." 1771.

"Compleat Joyner." 1772.

AMERICAN CRAFTSMEN

JOHN ELLIOTT, PHILADELPHIA

"In Chestnut Street at the corner of Fourth Street." Born at Bolton, Lancashire, England, June, 1713. Came to America in April, 1753. Died in 1791.

Cabinetmaker and maker of looking glasses, also importer of leather. Bill exists of 1754; advertiser in Philadelphia in 1756; removes in 1762 to Third and Walnut Streets.

His principal trade appears to have been in small pivoted dressing glasses on box bases, with drawers, of which several, with his label, have been found, also one or two wall mirrors.

JAMES GILLINGHAM, PHILADELPHIA

Born in Bucks County, Pennsylvania, 1736. His shop was in Second Street, Philadelphia, "a little below Dr. Thomas Bond's."

A good maker, his furniture being simple but of fine character.

JOHN GODDARD, NEWPORT, R. I.

Born Dartmouth, Massachusetts, January 20th, 1723 (4). Son of Daniel Goddard, a shipwright, and Mary Goddard (Tripp). John Goddard was apprenticed to a cabinetmaker and was free of the trade in 1744–5.

In 1782 he advertises in Providence "Goddard & Engs, Cabinetmakers from Newport, at their Shop on the wharf of Mr. Moses Brown, a little below Messrs. Tillinghart and Hoyroyd, near the Baptist Meeting House" which shows that he had removed from Newport at this date. John Goddard died at Newport, in July, 1785.

The block-front is the distinguishing feature of Goddard's work, but it is doubtful whether he made anything like all the work in this manner, which exists, of his period.

JONATHAN GOSTELOWE, PHILADELPHIA

Born Passayunk, 1745. Retired, 1793.

"At his Shop in Church Alley, about midway between Second and Third Streets"; removed to 68 Market Street in 1790, "The third house from the

Presbyterian Meeting House, between Second and Third Streets." Gostelowe's furniture, while of high quality, does not appear to bear any distinguishing characteristics. It follows the 1740–60 English models very closely, especially in the use of the ogee bracket-foot on chests and similar pieces.

SAMUEL McINTIRE, SALEM

Born, lived and died in Salem, 1757–1811.

It is doubtful that McIntire made furniture, but he was responsible for many of the fine house porches, and some carvings in Salem houses. He had a distinctive style and his work is of high quality, in craftsmanship, design and proportion.

THOMAS NATT, PHILADELPHIA

"192 Chestnut Street, near Eighth."

"Importer of British and French Looking Glasses."

DUNCAN PHYFE, NEW YORK

Born, 1768. Died, 1854.

The family came to America in 1783–4 from Loch Fannick, near Inverness, Scotland.

Duncan Phyfe commenced in Albany, when a boy of sixteen, and learned his trade there. He had a shop in New York, first at Broad Street, afterwards at 35 Partition Street (now the part of Fulton Street west of Broadway). In 1795 this was called Fair Street. In 1837 the style of the firm was D. Phyfe & Sons, in 1840 D. Phyfe & Son. Duncan Phyfe retired in 1847 and lived at 193 Fulton Street until his death in 1854. He was buried in Greenwood Cemetery, Brooklyn. Duncan Phyfe followed, almost exclusively, the English Empire style of the late Sheraton period. He had many imitators, but none appear to have copied him in the selection of fine timber, straight-grained dark Cuban mahogany, exceedingly close, hard and heavy. This wood necessitated a definite style of carving, almost akin to sculpture. When properly studied, Duncan Phyfe's work is unmistakable.

BENJAMIN RANDOLPH, PHILADELPHIA

An important maker, "At the Golden Eagle in Chestnut Street. Between Third and Fourth Streets." Advertisements of his engraved by J. Smither, in 1770, adapted from various plates in Chippendale's "Director." Advertises himself as a merchant in 1778, of glass, broadcloths, spices and tea.

A label of his is on a simple Chippendale chair in the Philadelphia Museum, but he is reputed to have made some fine chairs, in the full American-Chippendale manner, owned by Mr. Howard Reifsnyder, and was probably responsible for many of the fine Philadelphia "high-boys" of his period.

WILLIAM SAVERY, PHILADELPHIA

Born, 1720. Married in Philadelphia, 1746. Died, 1787.

His shop at "The Sign of the Chair in Second Street by Market Street" was on quite a small scale, being on a 12 ft. 6 in. lot. It is more than doubtful, therefore, that he could have made a tithe of the furniture which has been attributed to him.

His labels have been found in the top drawer of a "low-boy" at the Van Cortlandt Manor, also on two chairs of simple, crude Queen Anne type now in the Pennsylvania Memorial Hall, Philadelphia, on a fine walnut Queen Anne chair owned by Mr. Howard Reifsnyder, on a maple side chair of Dutch character owned by Mr. Addison H. Savery (a lineal descendant), and on a maple, slat-back chair (converted to a rocker at a later date) owned by Mr. Charles A. Raymond.

THOMAS TUFFT, PHILADELPHIA

Married in 1766; figures in Directory, 1785; died in the year of the plague, 1793.

Cabinet-and-chair-maker, "Four Doors from the Corner of Walnut Street in Second Street, Philadelphia."

His label recently found in a "low-boy" of simple, but good type.

(See "Antiques," Boston, October, 1927).

BIBLIOGRAPHY

BENN, Styles in Furniture. A history of furniture with over 100 full-page plates and numerous text illustrations.

BINSTEAD, English Chairs. With specimens illustrating the various periods from the 15th to the 19th century, 84 plates with over 300 examples.

CESCINSKY, Early English Furniture and Woodwork. Containing over 90 illustrations.

CESCINSKY, English Furniture of the Eighteenth Century. Containing over 1,200 illustrations from photographs and drawings of the best examples of the furniture of Hepplewhite, Sheraton, Adam, Chippendale, etc.

CESCINSKY, The Old World House, Its Furniture and Decoration. Containing examples of furniture and woodwork from Tudor days to the end of the 18th century, over 400 illustrations.

CHARLES, Old English Interiors.

CLIFFORD, Period Furnishings. An encyclopedia of historic furniture, decorations and furnishings.

CORNELIUS, Early American Furniture.

CORNELIUS, Furniture Masterpieces of Duncan Phyfe. Photographs and measured detail drawings.

DYER, Early American Craftsmen.

EBERLEIN, The Practical Book of Interior Decoration. With 460 pages of text, 300 illustrations of interiors and furniture, including 7 plates in color.

EBERLEIN & MCCLURE, The Practical Book of Period Furniture. Treating of the furniture of the English, American Colonial and Post-Colonial and principal French periods. Containing 250 illustrations and color plates and text illustrations from drawings by McClure.

ERNEST GIMSON, His Life and Work. Containing 60 collotype plates with over 100 illustrations of architectural plans, furniture and metal work.

FOLEY, The Book of Decorative Furniture, Its Form, Color and History. Containing 100 reproductions in full-color facsimile of drawings by the author and 1,000 text illustrations. Correlated charts of British woodwork styles and contemporaries, decorative furnishing accessories, principal trees, etc.

FRENCH, Colonial Interiors. Photographs and measured drawings of the Colonial and Early Federal periods.

GODFREY, The English Staircase. An historical account of its characteristic types to the end of the 18th century. Containing 63 collotype plates from photographs specially taken, with 55 text illustrations from sketches. Measured drawings and photographs.

HALSEY & CORNELIUS, Handbook of the American Wing of the Metropolitan Museum of Art, New York.

HOLLOWAY, The Practical Book of Furnishing the Small House and Apartment. With 9 illustrations in color, 198 in doubletone and 7 diagrams.

HUNTER, Decorative Furniture. A picture book of the beautiful forms of all ages and all periods, with more than 900 illustrations, 23 plates in color.

JACQUEMART, A History of Furniture. With numerous illustrations.

JOURDAIN, English Decoration and Furniture of the Early Renaissance (1500–1650). An account of its development and characteristic forms, containing over 400 illustrations of photographs and measured drawings.

JOURDAIN, English Decoration and Furniture of the Later XVIIIth Century (1760–1820). An account of its development and characteristic forms, containing over 400 illustrations of photographs and measured drawings.

JOURDAIN, English Interiors in Smaller Houses from the Restoration to the Regency (1660–1830). With over 200 illustrations of photographs and measured drawings.

KELLY, Early Connecticut Architecture. Measured drawings with full size details of moulded sections supplemented by photographs, 25 plates.

KELLY, The Early Domestic Architecture of Connecticut.

KIMBALL, Domestic Architecture of the American Colonies and of the Early Republic. Over 200 illustrations of photographs and plans.

LENYGON, Furniture in England from 1660–1760. With over 400 illustrations, of which 104 are full-page, printed in sepia tint from special photographs, 5 in colors.

LOCKWOOD, Colonial Furniture of America. With 867 illustrations of representative pieces.

LYON, Colonial Furniture of New England.

McCLELLAND, Historic Wall Papers.

MACQUOID, A History of English Furniture. From the beginning of Tudor times down to the last of the Georges. In four volumes each covering a separate period and complete in itself, viz.: The Age of Oak; The Age of Walnut; The Age of Mahogany; The Age of Satinwood. Illustrated with 1,000 large illustrations including 60 plates in color.

MACQUOID AND EDWARDS, The Dictionary of English Furniture. From the Middle Ages to the Late Georgian Period. Each of the three volumes contains upward of 500 illustrations from photographs with some few colored plates.

MAJOR, Domestic Architecture of the Early American Republic.

MILLAR, Colonial Furniture.

MILLAR, Some Colonial and Georgian Houses.

MOORE, The Old Furniture Book. With 112 illustrations.

MORSE, Furniture of the Olden Times. With 428 illustrations.

NASH, Mansions of England in the Olden Time.

NORTHEND, Historic Doorways of Old Salem.

NORTHEND, We Visit Old Inns.

NUTTING, American Windsors. All the various types illustrated.

NUTTING, Furniture of the Pilgrim Century. 1620–1720. Including Colonial utensils and hardware, illustrated with 1,000 photographs.

NYE, Colonial Furniture. A collection of scaled drawings. Fifty-five plates.

OSBURN, Measured Drawings of Early American Furniture.

PERCIVAL, Old English Furniture and Its Surroundings. From the Restoration to the Regency, profusely illustrated.

RAMSEY & HARVEY, Small Houses of the Late Georgian period.

SHUFFREY, The English Fireplace. A history of the development of the chimney-piece and firegrate, with their accessories, from the earliest times to the beginning of the 19th century. Illustrated by 130 full-page plates, reproduced in collotype from choice photographs, with 200 further illustrations in the text from sketches, measured drawings and photographs.

SINGLETON, Furniture of Our Forefathers.

STRANGE, English Furniture. Decoration, woodwork and allied arts, during the last half of the 17th century and the whole of the 18th and the earlier part of the 19th century. Over 1,000 illustrations.

STRATTON, The English Interior. A view of the decoration of English homes from Tudor times to the 19th century. Containing 115 plates and detailed drawings with numerous colored plates and over 75 illustrations in the text.

SWAN, Some 18th Century Designs for Interior Decorations.

TANNER, English Interior Woodwork of the Sixteenth, Seventeenth and Eighteenth Centuries. A series of 50 plates containing the best and most characteristic examples of chimney-pieces, paneling, staircases, doors, screens, etc. Measured and drawn and with introductory and descriptive text.

TIPPING, Grinling Gibbons and the Woodwork of His Age. 1648–1720. 620 pages with over 350 superb illustrations.

WARE, The Georgian Period. The most complete work on Colonial and Georgian architecture. Contains photographs and measured drawings.

WARE, The Students' Edition of the Georgian Period. 100 selected plates from "The Georgian Period."

www.ingramcontent.com/pod-product-compliance
Lightning Source LLC
Chambersburg PA
CBHW081134300726
48982CB00005B/966
9780983578499